# Crucible
# of Love

The Alchemy of Passionate Relationships

***For the guides***
'As above, so below'
and the Great Liberation


Love is a thyng as any spirit free.
Wommen, of kynde, desiren libertee,
And nat to been constreyned as a thral;
And so doon men, if I sooth seyen shal.

– Geoffrey Chaucer, 'The Franklin's Tale', *The Canterbury Tales*

# Crucible
# of Love

## The Alchemy of Passionate Relationships

### Jay Ramsay

BOOKS

Winchester, UK
Washington, USA

First published by O-Books, 2004
Second edition 2012
O-Books is an imprint of John Hunt Publishing Ltd., Laurel House, Station Approach,
Alresford, Hants, SO24 9JH, UK
office1@o-books.net
www.o-books.com

For distributor details and how to order please visit the 'Ordering' section on our website.

ISBN: 978 1 78099 203 7

Design: Stuart Davies

Printed in the UK by CPI Antony Rowe

We operate a distinctive and ethical publishing philosophy in all
areas of our business, from our global network of authors to
production and worldwide distribution.

# CONTENTS

# Acknowledgements

To Joy and Bob Redfield Kwapien, and Treasa O'Driscoll: if we hadn't met in Dublin this would never have been possible, despite everything...

To Daisy Tufnell and 'the team' for their invaluable guidance.

To all the many friends and strangers who said or suggested just the right thing at the right time: and especially—

To Lizzie Hutchins, my editor and friend, for lifting its essence clear and cheering it on.

To Helen Elwes for embodying alchemy in her fine and inspired illustrations.

To Liz Puttick, my agent and friend, for her unfailing encouragement and rigour.

To Ian Fenton and Mary Ashwin for their double pelican.

To Michael Mann for his on-going support of poetry at a prosaic time.

To Margaret Marion Stewart for her unparalleled clear seeing.

To Susie, for suffering it – and for her radiant clear lightning.

And to You for showing us that *love is eternal life.*

# Prelude

*Love is where we came from. Love is why we're here. Love is where we're going to.*

*In the beginning that has no end, there was love.*

*Before words. Before action. Before thought as we knew it.*

*There was beingness: the fusion of creation and matter with itself.*

*And it is in us, deep in our bodies. You can see it, shining in our eyes.*

*In the beginning, before we came here, when we were together in soul, there was love. And the beginning is where we return to, where we end.*

*Love is the work, love is the return.*

*So why do we come here at all?*

*To learn to love, under the most difficult circumstances of all. To bring, to birth love. And to further love – knowing it is at the heart of our evolution as a species. Our only evolution is love.*

*And when we have achieved that, when we have finally opened ourselves – we die. When we have done what we can with this mortal body and our mortal minds. It may only be in the last invisible seconds of our passing...*

*And then we are released to where our journey takes us on. To where there are new horizons and where we have new choices.*

*Because the Kingdom of Love is vast. It encompasses everything. The way earth meets sky, and sky expands the earth in its rolling sea of cloud and blue...*

*Love is where we came from. Love is why we're here. Love is where we're going to.*

# FOREWORD

Wherever we turn these days it seems we are confronted by the problem of how to reconcile the apparently irreconcilable opposing forces that threaten to tear our lives apart. Whether in the Middle East or in Northern Ireland, whether on the contested border zones of the planet or in the suddenly vulnerable target-cities of both hemispheres, year in year out we see our failure to address the difficult and urgent issues posed by the problem dramatised in almost daily images of violence, suffering and destruction.

Nor do we need to venture into the wider political arena to see how incompetent we are at enduring, and transforming, the tensions that our own complex, contrary nature sets up between and inside us. Racial and cultural divisions, the conflicts that torment broken families, the anguish of individual minds caught in the conflicting demands of emotional double-binds - all are the intolerable consequence of our failure to complete the hard journey that might take us between the clashing rocks, through an honest admission of our differences, and on to a place of creative reconciliation.

Too often seen merely as an erroneous precursor to modern science, alchemy was, at its most sophisticated, a heart-felt attempt to approach a solution to this problem through an experimentally applied effort of the intellectual imagination. Whether they claimed to be in quest of the Philosopher's Stone, the Elixir of Life or the Panacea for all ills, as they pored over their books or sweated at their furnaces the old adepts were looking to bring the contrary aspects of the human soul and the material world into fruitful new relation. Their ambition – though the word does no justice to the spiritual humility with which the best of them applied themselves to their endeavours – was to accomplish and celebrate the *Mysterium Coniunctionis,* that difficult and elusive reconciliation of opposing principles which is the means -I think, the *only* means- by which something new gets made for life.

It's not surprising, therefore, that certain aspects of the alchemical drama should have manifested themselves in imagery drawn from our sexuality - though it would be a grave mistake simply to reduce the mystery to that level. The copulating kings and queens who are the protagonists of 'the Royal Art' were emblems of archetypal powers which range far beyond the delights and conflicts of the marriage bed, so it would be a further mistake to conceive of them solely in psycho-logical terms. But at a time when gender relations remain, by and large, in a drastic state of misprision, and when we have only a dim sense of the way in which the outward conflicts of literal gender mirror the inward conflicts of both men and women, alchemy offers an illuminating vocabulary of images to help us recognise what is going on.

For many years now, as both therapist and teacher, Jay Ramsay has applied his poet's imagination to working with the language of alchemy. His new book is a kind of alchemical crucible in which we can watch the erotic aspects of its drama played out for our time. It offers us a personal vision of how the images of alchemy may still be of vital service in coming to understand what we are talking about when we talk about love.

Lindsay Clarke

Introduction

# The Crisis and the Opportunity

Without love, humanity could not exist for a day
– Erich Fromm

Love is our birthright, deep in the cells of our bodies. Love is our most natural state, it is the most natural place in the world to be – when we are in it. But we are not used to being in it. Our normal state is one of distance, and distance breeds a particular distortion, a negative seeing and a negative expectation of any stranger: our first reaction is more likely to be enmity than openness. That distance is one we have to cross. It is our wound, our sickness and our abyss.

So, we are in crisis. The vessel of our world is simmering over an invisible fire. But do we know what this crisis is? We can think of it materially as a crisis of resources and ecologically as a crisis of survival, but if we can think of it essentially in terms of relationship, we can see that above all *it is a crisis of feeling*. A crisis of feeling, disabled by fear.

The fear stems from our alienation and distance. We are afraid to feel, afraid that we will be rejected, that we will be alone, unable to survive. We are constantly trying to insure ourselves against abandonment and pain. However, because this goes against the spirit of life, it creates a contraction in which our own spark is stifled. We lose the energy to break out, to be spontaneous, fluid and mobile as feeling itself is. We become rigid, not so much living *in* form as subsumed *by* it, while at the same time persuading ourselves and each other that this is, after all, reality. But this reality is breaking down.

Our need for love, and to understand love, has never been

4

greater than now. The problems confronting us make us realize that we literally cannot survive without it. The Greek word for 'crisis' also means 'opportunity'. This is our opportunity.

\* \* \* \* \*

As a Tina Turner song asked, 'What's love got to do with it?' I took it as a provocative question. 'Everything,' I wanted to say every time I heard the refrain. And it set me thinking.

As I looked around, my first point of reference was the relationships in front of me, which increasingly, it seemed, were not working. All too often, the relationships seemed smaller than the sum of the two people involved. Couples I knew were constantly at odds with each other, in frozen denial, moving apart or actually separating, until everywhere I looked I seemed to be seeing a version of the same thing: *relationships as we've known them are no longer working.*

I found myself asking, 'Where is the passion, the generosity, the forgiveness, the breadth?' Love can change our entire perception of the world, but the love we know seems to be isolated, limited and impermanent.

At the same time I started to notice something else. It wasn't simply that we weren't any good at relationships – there was more to it than that. There was a reason why they were being apparently subverted – and not simply so we could find more ingenious ways of patching them up. Something deeper and more troubling was going on. *We were being invited – or even forced – to see relationships in a new light.*

That is where this book began, ten years or so ago now, with an undefined but increasingly urgent sense that a structure we knew (or thought we knew) was going to have to change. And there was alchemy. While researching my previous book,[1] I realized that far from being an obscurely pictured mediaeval system, alchemy not only has so much to say to us today about wholeness, imagination and healing, but does so specifically about man–woman relationship as key to its process – a journey and initiation through death and rebirth, separation and reunion, where both partners are changed and can attain their true or 'royal' potential.

Inspired by Jung's work,[2] which took alchemy seriously as psychological and transformative reality, I was excited by the therapeutic possibilities as well as the amazing creativity and poetry inherent within it. So, with seeds and hints of this present book in my previous one, it became the natural framework and 'flask' (or container) for this exploration.

At the same time I was questioning everything. Were couples a thing of the past, still lingering on? How could marriages exist and meaningfully survive? What did it mean to love more than one person? How could we open to a greater loving in which we could genuinely grow in freedom? These were the questions, I felt, that we were being invited to ask. This was how we were being invited to see relationships. And not just from our own convenient view, emotionally or intellectually, but *from spirit*. That was where the change was coming.

* * * * *

Alchemy is a word that has resurfaced recently in our general awareness. Most of us know it has to do with turning base metal (or lead) into gold and that it began in Egypt as an experimental laboratory process that increasingly - after the Renaissance - became a metaphor for our own inward being and *its* process. But what most of us don't know is that the alchemical process is basically about a man and a woman – Sol, the masculine, and Luna, the feminine – and that it has everything to say about relationships: our coming together, our separating, our reuniting, and all the work we are quickened into doing to keep the relationship alive and moving – that is, if we choose to.

Understanding alchemy in this inner sense helps us to deepen our relationships from a personality or ego level to a level of soul and spirit. And because alchemy sees relationship *as a process* rather than something to be simply 'fixed' when it goes wrong, it makes us less afraid of our difficulties: the difficulties between us and the difficult parts we all have in us. From an alchemical point of view it is precisely these difficulties that – with engagement rather than denial – can be openings to greater awareness, sensitivity and aliveness in its labour of transmutation and transformation.

The work of alchemy essentially takes place in a contained vessel, also referred to as a flask, a retort, an alembic. We can understand this container metaphorically as a safe space that allows us to open up to greater intensity, intimacy and creativity. This is the fire or 'heat' of the process. We also need containment, a safe and sacred space, to be able to open to our own higher level of awareness. So the flask is basic, and we each need to take responsibility for it. The opposite of containment in this sense is chaos and in extreme cases, psychosis.

*The flask*

Among the many illustrations of laboratory equipment, we also find the 'double pelican' — literally, two connected flasks — which specifically relates to the couple who do the work. This is both the alchemist and his female or male co-worker (the soror mystica or frater mysterium) and, inwardly, our alchemical lovers: Sol and Luna.

Alchemy also involves a third person or body who accompanies Sol and Luna at every stage: the ever-present, every-shifting, ever-changing Mercurius, who is both instinctual and spiritual, androgynous (or 'hermaphrodite') and bisexual. He is both genders and more. He points to us each having unique gender; we are all composed of masculine *and* feminine – and are not simply, so to speak, from Mars *or* Venus. And in relationship to Sol and Luna, we may imagine him like this moving between the shadow beneath them and the light above them:

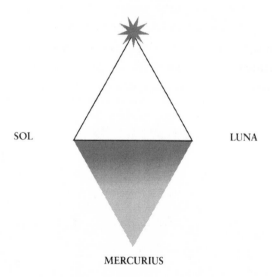

Alchemy is traditionally based on a heterosexual expression, but it is also about the masculine and feminine in all of us, which is why it shows Mercurius as androgynous and bisexual. Its calls us as men and women to open to our contrasexual (i.e. our 'other sex') nature, and it affirms our sexuality as bisexual (containing both) and fluid. Our sexuality changes through our lifetime as a mirror of our wholeness and what we need to experience as a result of our sexual persuasion at any time. If you are in a gay or lesbian relationship, you can read the journey of Sol and Luna for yourself, with your partner as the other sex. While both of you will be Sol (men) or Luna (women), the other sex journey will also be relevant in terms of what gender you feel you inhabit in relationship to your partner. Gay or lesbian relationships both emphasize a love of their own male or femaleness, physically experienced. Our own sexual nature inwardly as a man or woman not only contains the other gender, but points towards a condition of *unique gender* in each of us as individuals.

As an art and a science, alchemy is a spiritual process of transformation that reaches deep into matter, through our bodies. That means it includes our mental processes, our feelings and imagination, as well as our physical being, our sexuality and instinct. It is a truly holistic process and its goal is wholeness; the gold it creates is a quality of enlightenment in the body that is about being *here* in this world, fully awake, alive and loving.

Alchemical gold is not material gold. But it is no less real. We can think of its gold as being made of light and darkness, and requiring the existence of each. Relationships, it says, need both our light and darkness – our love, our vision and our difficulty and pain – if gold is to be formed between us.

And it is in and through this that alchemy sees that our relationships, like journeys, have a life of their own that are guided by what goes beyond us – however we name or understand that.

Alchemy, which opened the doors to the unconscious hundreds of years before Freud and psychology came into being, and which was wisely championed by C. G. Jung in his pioneering *Psychology and Alchemy*, is a therapeutic process and a spiritual path. It brings the psychological and the spiritual together, which is another aspect of its relevance for us today.

9

The stages of 'the Work' or *opus*, like chapters with their sections and sub-sections, have a profound natural logic that makes sense to our emotional rather than rational being, to our creative intuition as opposed to our intellect. The alchemical process has an unfolding 'rightness', then, as people I know who have experienced it (also in my workshops) have stated time and again. The sense is often of coming to recognize something – an event or phrase of one's life – in a new way that is also meaningful. 'Ah, that's what was happening – I see it now.'

Alchemy also takes us beyond what we know into new ground as well as deepened ground, just as intimate relationships do, where love is our path.

This book is that path. So taking alchemy as 'inner alchemy' where we are the process, I have mapped each of the main stages, applying them in detail to relationships and the issues that come up for us in them that challenge us to deepen, to shed our skins, to open our hearts and to extend our boundaries – above all, to journey from a love we know that is conditional towards a love we are beginning to know and need to discover (now more than ever) that is *un*conditional, that 'is' itself and that is greater than anything we have ever known.

So I begin with the love we know: falling in love in *conuinctio* (which means 'joining' or 'coming together'). Relationships as we know are (hopefully) wonderful in the beginning, but that isn't where they remain. In alchemy, this takes us to the *nigredo* (which means 'blackening'), where we discover our partners are not all we want them to be, which is where the difficulty that is also the death of the ego begins. *Nigredo* is the hardest part of the process. But our story is still only beginning. We then move into the softening and whitening realm of *solutio* ('solving', as in solution), with its emphasis on the soul itself freed from the control of the ego personality; with feeling, with the feminine (it is Luna's realm) and with purification. These two stages together complete the first part of the work.

We then cross over into what alchemy calls 'the Greater Work', which is where we really grow up (as well as down) into adulthood and where we spiritually awaken. In *coagulatio* (which literally means 'coagulation', with its connotation of grounding as well as thickening), we learn what it means to be separate people who need to stand on their own and find the other in themselves – in other words, as men, finding the feminine in ourselves, and as women, finding the masculine in ourselves. As well as seeing our partner(s) on their *own* path of development, that is their soul's individuality, this also opens us up to the realm of the 'inner marriage' which is absolutely vital if any enduring 'outer marriage' is to take place or be sustained.

At the same time during this longest of our four main stages, I introduce and debate some of the key questions I have already mentioned. What does being in a couple mean? What does freedom mean within this? What holds our relationship together then? These include what I call 'erotic soul relationships' and also the challenges of community in extending our horizons of love and loving.

That greater dimension is the realm of the last stage, the *rubedo* (with its connotations of ruby as well as red and rose), with its rainbow bridge linking heaven and Earth which 'makes whole' again – and which is also the place where alchemy places the wedding which has been prepared and worked for. This alchemical or 'chymical' wedding is the true joining of our couple after all they have been through. It is the conscious as opposed to the unconscious marriage. And it is here too, as we will see, that we can understand that marriage is also about connecting the *whole* of life – facing outwards together and not just inwards – and ultimately the whole of the world, seen and unseen. Here we are awake and alive, in connection and 'in relationship' (rather than out of it), and this aliveness, this vitality, is part of what alchemy means by 'gold' as an awakened and enlightened state. It is also where a tremendous self-renewing energy called the Elixir of Life becomes available, as well as the magic and wisdom that alchemy famously calls 'the Philosopher's Stone' It is here too as men and women that we can fulfil something of our true potential – royal as we are as kings and queens in our true spiritual (and human) being.

And we must take the journey to find out.

The various suggestions and exercises at the end of each chapter are designed to encourage you in this both individually and in your relationship(s). My suggestion is that you work with them sequentially either over a period of time (while you read this book), or else focus on a particular area, having read it through, according to where you feel you are with your partner at this time.

It is useful to remember that where *you* may be individually is not where your relationship is. Equally your partner may also be individually at a different stage from you - this may also be what attracted you. However your *relationship* - and its 'third body' that you make together - will be identifiably at one and each of these stages. The 'double pelican' is a useful image to retain and reflect on here in terms of the structure of what follows, and how you understand and work with it.

To summarize and also introduce then, to end and begin at the same time, here is a map of the serpentine journey you are about to make ... and perhaps not for the first time:

light, recognition
first love, falling in love
*conuinctio*
**'the relationship we recognize'**

into the Black
descending
*nigredo*
**'the relationship we dread'**

Whitening
purifying
*solutio*
**'the relationship we dream of'**

Yellowing/Green
grounding
*coagulatio*
separation, differentiation
(the Desert Journey)
**'the relationship we fear and resist'**

Reddening/Purple/Gold
union, synthesis
('as above, so below')
the Wedding
*rubedo*
**'love's relationship with us'**

ouroboros
(the great snake)
the end that is the beginning
 of a new cycle

# Part One

# The Lesser Work: Coniunctio, Nigredo and Solutio

Chapter One

# When Love Goes to Hell

*conuinctio* – falling in love
*nigredo* – ego death
'the relationship we dread'

For there can be no love story unless love meets with
opposition.
– Denis de Rougemont

If we don't know what love is, or cannot conceive of what it could
mean, one way of beginning is to look at what love *is not*. This
also applies to our experience of identity. Many of us don't know
who we are – we may know more about *what we are not*. As T. S.
Eliot wrote:

In order to arrive at what you are not
You must go through the way in which you are not.[1]

That is a journey for ourselves, and for our experience of love,
that bears its own potent fruit.

## What Love Is Not

Some of what love is not is so obvious it hardly needs stating. In
an article in a mainstream British newspaper, published just
before Christmas, a large photograph shows the first stages of a
Hollywood-filmed Roman orgy, and underneath the heading
'Usual rules suspended', it begins:

'We ran into the toilet and I took her against the wall, while the fairy lights bobbed outside the window and tinsel fell from her hair.'

Tales of lust abound at this time of year.[2]

Not tales of love, it would seem. At least, not reported here. A little further on in the same newspaper, in the arts section, a colour photograph of a new piece of sculpture-cum-montage called *State of the Art* shows a skyline of consumer durables – lipsticks, small portable radios, vibrators and other sex aids, plastic toys and skulls – against a featureless red neon smog. It is a fitting testament to where we are, to what we have created: narcissism and materialist self-obsession on a grand scale, grand as Manhattan. It is the fantasy of freedom we inhabit, a machine that runs on constant stimulation. We could call it hell: a city that never sleeps or subsides. This is one way of looking at it.

Love is not sex, though it can come through sex, transforming it from something cinematic and hard-edged into itself. Love is not fantasy, any more than it is a passing fancy for a stranger on the street. *Love is not a disconnected image in our heads.*

But let us not be too sure. We are in a realm of extremes here, as well as a realm of illusion. At the other extreme is the story of romantic love – or rather, one version of that story that has become accepted throughout Western culture. And we must understand the negative side of that story before we can release the positive aspects that have been, like the proverbial baby, thrown out with the bath water.

This archetypal story in itself is simple. A knight meets a lady who is unavailable (married, usually) and both fall in love, intoxicated as if by a drug. We say they *fall* in love, which is a convenient phrase that covers falling also in lust, or repressed passion, for a quality that neither of them has in their lives. Both of them see this quality in each other – they *must* see it, because their lives depend on it. Both are looking *out* of themselves towards the one they love. Or are they? Are they actually seeing the other person?

Denis de Rougemont would say not:

> Tristan and Iseult do not love each other. They say they don't, and everything goes to prove it. *What they love is love and being in love...* Tristan loves the awareness he is loving much more than he loves Iseult the Fair. And Iseult does nothing to hold Tristan. All she needs is her passionate dream.[3]

This kind of passion is one that leads the lovers away from the world, away from reality on a one-way trip; and ultimately as the story itself describes, into death as the only possible resolution.

This courtly medieval story of Tristan and Iseult is completely familiar, as it has continued across time, entering popular culture in a million comparable romances. The dress and occupation have changed, the essence has not. To this day love is still coupled with unreality, in fact even more so for having lost its inspirational origin:

> He smiled down at her and she realized how tall he was, and for that matter, how good looking. But his dark sunburned face with high, rather prominent cheekbones, deep-set, dark eyes and a square forehead all seemed somehow unimportant beside his smile. In fact, there was no doubt about it, his smile was irresistible.[4]

From Tristan and Iseult to the clichés of Harlequin or Mills & Boon, what we have are stories that obstruct the *real* story in all its passion and substance. Love in this form is based solely on projection and image, not on seeing and allowing the other to be as he or she is. It is also based on the impossibility of an actual relationship taking place. It cannot be otherwise. And why is that ? If it were, our view of love itself would have to change.

## The Myth of Love

It is the story behind the veil of the traditional romantic story that concerns us here, but what we first have to recognize is that it is this story that has created the *status quo* of the love we know, the love we dream of, the love that is acceptable. I call this 'the myth of love' and it forms the basis of the couple we recognize, as well as conventional marriage at any rung of the social ladder.

In this story a familiar and often unconscious set of expectations is created of the romance from the beginning. Our lover is seen as an extension of ourselves – our 'other half' – and as our protector against pain, abandonment and death. Our lover is also exclusive to us in the institution we know as monogamy, which guarantees us a semblance of security outside ourselves. Our lover is placed *between* us and life. Where we were one, we are now two. The world out there is secondary, and beyond the immediate circle of chosen friends (or other couples) and family is a place composed of strangers and potential enemies. Who, after all, could compare with our loved one? Who could we possibly think of opening ourselves to in the same way?

In this view, what do we see? There is no concept of any relationship *with ourselves*, a relationship that is primary, coming before any relationship we have with anyone else. We have never been taught this. Instead we believe (especially when we are in love) that our lover finally and miraculously 'completes' us.

As a result we also lack an adequate sense of our lover *as other* – as mysterious (however familiar), uncontrollable and beyond our reckoning. There is no concept of the *freedom of the other* as something basic and necessary. So, the other's needs can often become unrecognized, buried, suppressed, compromised. We enter a 'pact of twoness' where the relationship becomes a possession rather than a gift, with all its attendant spoken or unspoken restrictions. What do we find ? We learn to behave accordingly, with good and bad behaviour rewarded in kind.

Love here thinly masks its own other, which is power.

What is interesting and sad is to see how frequently, in this account of 'two and two only', the couple as a unit becomes distorted: frustrated, unhappy or simply disconnected from life. There are two extremes here: at one end of the scale is the romanticized *folie à deux* of headlong headstrong honeymoon lovers; at the other is the couple 'team' running their relationship like an office, rather than (perhaps) as an entity constantly in need of attention, consciousness and renewal. And how close these two ends of the spectrum are in reality, when honeymoon becomes marriage with its vow of fidelity.

A *folie à deux* can, however, take many forms. One is the shadow of exclusivity, which is isolation and selfishness. Nadia and James, for instance, live next door to Mary. They know Mary has lost her job and they know she is distressed, unsupported and anxious about money, but they haven't called her or called round to see her. Why? Because James has just flown in to see Nadia from the other side of the globe and they are in love.

Lovers need space to connect to their own space. However, notice the priority here: *we first, you later. We now, you when we feel like it.* The couple here is superior to the single person, who is left out in the cold as the two stay warm. And this is generally acceptable.

Another distortion, after the selfish couple, is the rigid couple. The rigid couple are set in their ways and despite being unhappy, hang onto the structure they have made out of their unresolved issues. Neither of them is willing to face change and yet neither of them is willing to really acknowledge their need of each other. Both stay shackled in a repetitive cycle of conflict, both are impeded, and they are getting older all the time.

Rigidity is what sets in when the space between two people goes unrecognized. It is like a kind of emotional arthritis: it is painful and seemingly insoluble. It rationalizes its own pain. Mostly it is something which is regarded as unfortunate but likely in a long-term relationship. People who thrive over a long period of time together are 'lucky', as if by some random lottery selection. We don't question the rigidity of the rigid couple. At best we salute them for 'staying with it'.

Thirdly, there is also the single person who behaves with the expectation of being in a couple. Such a person is jealous and possessive towards the person he or she wants to be with. He, in this example, asks for her friend's phone number. They have all recently met in a pub. She reacts with jealous insecurity. 'But we all met together,' he protests. And still she refuses to give it to him. He finally gives up. This is not a promising beginning! Yet her reaction, in our world of glossy magazine short stories, is supposedly acceptable and understandable. She wants *him* and therefore doesn't want *her friend* to talk to him. This is the logic we recognize. He, on the other hand, consciously or not, is already feeling manipulated and coerced. Love is shrinking by the second. Freedom is not being allowed. A bad seed has already been sown.

A fourth example is of an 'ex-couple'. This is connected to the issue of letting go, which is another way we need to see the space between two people. Dennis and Jill have finally separated after an agonizing two-year period during which, after many other brief affairs, he has been with a younger woman who is his secretary. But he has not been able to make up his mind, while Jill has been suffering, unable to take a stand. Finally she decides she will not see him for a time. She also begins a new relationship with a younger man. This immediately draws Dennis back to her, declaring his love and saying he has definitely 'made a mistake'. There is no other woman like her and he will end his liaison with his secretary (to whom he has already proposed) at once.

Dennis has been dishonest with Jill. He is still being dishonest, with himself. What he is calling love is actually his need for a lifestyle in which he felt safe. It doesn't really have anything to do with Jill as she was or as she is now. It is his grief about what has been. Dennis and Jill are trying to negotiate a new stage of relationship. But for that to take place, they both have to *let go* of what has been, as well as express their hurt feelings honestly. The lack of honesty makes a relationship between them impossible – yet at the same time the space between them demands it.

## The Third Body

What all of this points to is the nature of this space between people that I have been alluding to. Robert Bly, in a memorable phrase, calls it the 'third body' and it points to a central truth here which is vital for our purposes: *there are never two merely people in a relationship, there are always three.* This third person, body or being is *love*. It is the specific energy and intelligence of the space between the two people, a constellation that is unique to each couple and each relationship. And just as each relationship is different, each has a different purpose that is as individual as we are. We could even say that each relationship has its own destiny, which is also unique to it, and which we only partly know.

Bly's phrase is suggestive, precise and useful in his inclusion of the word 'body'. It is a poetic phrase and it carries the tension of something that is simultaneously present and invisible, numinous and substantial. This is how I evoked it in a prose poem in my previous book, *Alchemy:*

> ...this other body that they make as they love, this body that they leave and return to as it grows
>
> silently in the in-between space of them.[5]

It is like a ghost that is light – and not on the other side or in the borderlands immediately after death, but *here*, in life. It is the presence of spirit between us, in what we know or perhaps suddenly realize in a flash of intuition – 'That's it! That's what we need to do!' And it is of the soul, too, pointing deep into the body, felt through intimacy and love-making (if the relationship is sexual), and 'growing' in time as our contact with each other develops.

It is also useful to think of it as being like the apex of a triangle, with the two people in a relationship as the points at its base. To bring in an analogy from philosophy, it is the point of synthesis that supersedes thesis and antithesis in a leap beyond to a third point. It is above us, around us, under us, within and between us. And however we define it (and part of its nature is that it will not be pinned down like a collected butterfly) we can say that it has an intelligence, a will and an agenda of its own. That is, when we are open to it – or even if we are not...

What we need to see here is that when there is a failure to recognize the spirit of any relationship (in any form), dysfunction is the result. The failure to recognize the third body of a relationship is also reflected in what happens when a third actual person comes into the arena of a couple. This may be another lover, whatever that might actually mean for the relationship, but it may not be another adult at all, it may equally be a baby, which means the relationship between the couple also has to change. And as the mother bonds with the baby, the father can feel equally estranged, plunged back into the needy infant inside himself, sometimes with negative consequences.

What are the implications of this? It is surely an invitation to see our relationships as spiritual and soulful entities, not merely as possessions under our will and direction. We need to do this if we are to have relationships that actually function and bring joy, serving their hidden and even miraculous purpose. It is, I believe, a necessity in our evolving process. But we have to come to see our relationships in a new way. The new wine will not fit in the old bottles. And the bottles, it would seem, are breaking anyway.

## The Myth of Love Clarified

This recognition brings us to an understanding of what the myth of love is. And it is simply this: *that it is ours to possess and control.* But this is not the reality. Love is not a possession, like a car or a chainsaw. It is a gift and, as we very well know, it can be given and taken – and not apparently voluntarily. It can withdraw of itself.

Furthermore, the myth of love, or romantic love, as we have understood it in the last eight centuries, *is that our lover is the Beloved.* However we understand the Beloved, the confusion here is central. *No one human being can be the Beloved*, the be-all and end-all. Beloved, yes, much loved, of course, but never *the* Beloved. That belongs to Love alone. So much of our pain and tragedy lies in our basic refusal to recognize this. We cling on to each other precisely when we need to let go and open out to the greater being that holds us as well as flowing through us. And it is only when we do so that we can really be together as we were made to be. Not that it is easy, because our journey, like all journeys worth their while, involves many obstacles, both within ourselves and from our past.

So in the myth of love *we confuse the lover with Love* and not only with Love as a more abstract entity, *but with the love inside us as well,* and the relationship we need to begin having with ourselves. Time and again, the same reality emerges: we discover to our dismay that love is based not on itself, but on fear; not on rock, but on raging sand.

And what then?

* * * * *

Sometimes it seems as if the only way we can look at relationships is in terms of right and wrong. If the relationship is right, it's OK, smile and be happy, ring your friends. If it's wrong, then we had better fix it, and the sooner the better. We don't like the pain. This has spawned a plethora of books that basically address what is *wrong* with relationships and how we can make them *right*. Many of these books contain useful and insightful things, but there is something inevitably superficial about looking at what connects us to each other in this way. It is as if all the complexity, the magic and hard-won poetry can be reduced to a series of bullet points like a supermarket shopping list – as if all we were doing was going shopping anyway. It is only when something goes 'wrong' that we bother to look at it more closely. We can take it for granted otherwise. While it is 'wrong' we are seeing more deeply into it – and it is revealing something deeper to us.

What we lack above all in our conception of relationships is a sense of *process* that recognizes that what is 'wrong' (or difficult, or painful) also has to be there.

And this is where alchemy is so relevant to us now.

## Coniunctio

Alchemy recognizes the romantic first stage of relationship as vital. It is what brings the lovers together. But it is only the beginning. Boy meets girl, *puer* meets *puella*, man meets woman, and potential king meets potential queen. The romance of the beginning is the falling in love. *At last I have found someone I feel totally connected to,* we may say. And she is not only woman, but she is sister and she is sexual sister (or brother) as well. And she is not only outside me, but inside me. She is other and she feels like me. She is here, where before there was only a dream. She's here!

This is the light we meet in, and it can be literally like light moving between us. It is as if something is being made plain. We can't easily avoid it.

This leads to what alchemy calls the *coniunctio* (literally 'conjunction' or 'joining'), where the lovers celebrate their recognition by having sex. More than that, because the sex feels right, it *is* right, it is love – and it feels like heaven. Everything comes alive, is rejuvenated. Everything is possible again. And out of this comes the vision and potential we can share, glittering like sunlight on water or the first flush of dawn.

*Her eyes like roses as she leaned on his shoulder and looked into his own as if to say, 'I know – do you?'*

All of this is true. And it is going to have to change. Because it is only the beginning, even though it seems it will last. It is not an illusion, nor is it all projection, although of course projection is there, because projection is always involved when we relate. He is seeing his feminine in her and she is seeing her masculine in him, and the fit is perfect. But that feminine and that masculine are going to call the couple deeper into their relationship and deeper into themselves as well. Because our contrasexual selves (the woman in a man and the man in a woman) also come partly from pain, which in turn comes from our past. Our images of both come from our parents, in what they have represented, and in the distorted as well as limited ways they may have related to us. For instance, if a boy is told 'big boys don't cry' that will restrict his relationship to his feelings, and so to the feminine inside him. Equally if a girl is not fathered positively, she will grow up without a self-organizing masculine ability, tending towards dependency and chaos. There are many permutations here, also of course in how our *own* gender has been modelled to us by the first man or woman in our lives.

So the *coniunctio* is light for the coming darkness and for when the going gets tough, recognizing (as we may do) that we are going to be with our partner's shadow as well as their light. *Coniunctio* is ours to cherish, then; we are fools to throw it away. Without its light and height we could not go deeper; without its hope, who would want to? The problem is that as a culture we try and prolong this stage and when it naturally – usually with its own subtle warning signals – begins to draw to a close, we panic. We want it all back. So, when things start to go 'wrong', the process of patching up begins. But love is not lipstick in a mortuary. It knows what it is doing. And we need to get beyond this stage if our relationship is to go further.

## Into the Black

So we pass from the relationship we know to the relationship we dread. We dread it because this is where everything seems to go wrong. Alchemy calls this *nigredo*. It is associated with the colour black and, because alchemy has always had connections with astrology as well as different metals, the planet Saturn—who rules structure and form—as well. The *nigredo* is to do with a dying and a Dark Night that has to take place before there can be a rebirth. This dying is of the egoic, controlling, superficial part of ourselves that prevents us from connecting to the soul, that stands in the way of our own deeper, more feeling being.

We can recognize *nigredo* easily enough. It is everywhere in our culture at the present time, out there in the darkness. But we resist it, especially in a relationship, which is the one place we understandably want sweetness, light and safety. This is understandable, but not ultimately productive. It means we can't get to the soul of the relationship, which is where its healing takes place.

It takes courage to open to *nigredo*. But we may find we don't have a lot of choice in the matter anyway. Sooner or later our exclusively romantic images of each other run out of energy. With the best will in the world we can try to be ideal for each other, trying to please beyond our means. Yet who we really are and what we could really become together lie waiting underneath.

*He knew, or sensed this, as they lay in the summer field together. There was something else under her smiling and carefree-sounding laughter, and his own as well, like a shadow behind the sunlight, calling them deeper.*

In *Getting the Love You Want*, Harville Hendrix makes the point that we are not deeply attracted to people for the reasons we think we are. As a result of our past experience with parents and family – especially our fathers and mothers as our primary caretakers – we build up an 'imago', or composite image, which is made up of them and the parts of ourselves that we have repressed. We then project this onto our partners. As he says:

> This special person can't be just anyone. It can't be the first man or woman who comes along with an appealing smile or warm disposition. It has to be someone who stirs within us a deep sense of recognition: 'This is the one I've been looking for!' 'This is the one who will make up for the wounds of the past!'[6]

Mostly we are not aware of this, because it seems to point in the opposite direction from the sense of freedom in which we first come together. The last thing we initially feel is connected to our past. But that is not what our unconscious feels. It is looking precisely to heal those wounds. And the reality is we are all, to whatever extent, wounded. It is what writes us into the script of being human. To that extent, *nigredo* catches us unawares.

The irony is that *for those wounds to be healed they have, in the first place, to be re-evoked.* The exactness of this can be truly uncanny. It is a side of love we don't usually see or credit – the love that is science as well as art.

Another name for it is alchemy.

## Sol and Luna

In the *nigredo*, Sol and Luna, our alchemical couple, begin to
fight. We can hear their raised voices as a full-blown row coming
through the wall, or as we walk down the street, and it is said
that they (metaphorically) 'fight to the death'. The *nigredo*
reverses the *conuinctio* in every sense. It is also a metaphor for the
ego or lead – the heavy metal in us – being melted down,
bubbling and spitting as it does. This is what the fighting is
about.

*They have had an amazing drive down. Great clouds fringing the*
*horizon, like fragments of God's imagination, and a wide expansive*
*sky; his hand holding hers lightly off the wheel. And in the pub, as he*
*asks her what she feels about what women really want, there's another*
*conversation to remember, things she's said staying in his head. Later,*
*they go to bed.*

*She has been asking for space sexually, but somehow he hasn't heard*
*it. And in a way the message hasn't been clear from her either. She has*
*been so available, after all, all these months. The imprint of her body is*
*etched in his desire. And this is their holiday, rare time together.*

*Then in the middle of the night, he wakes suddenly, feeling warm*
*towards her. She wakes then, but it's as if they've both woken at the*
*same time. It seems to him as if she wants him. But she feels pressured.*
*She feels anger unstoppably rising...*

The impact is shattering, as we know. Suddenly we seem to be
with someone we *don't* know, the air taking us further apart with
every word we utter, the tension making touch impossible. Here
the *conuinctio* reverses, the dream of union collapses, and with it
the images we have had where we have been like a prince and
princess. We fall out of grace – and is it into hell or simply to
earth? It is both.

In this we are confronted with all of our difference, which is another beginning or awakening, but one which finds us angry, hurting and afraid. And hating this. Wanting to get away. Wanting to be anywhere else. Likely as not, there won't be anywhere to go to – for all our freedom, there is suddenly no escape. And we may choose to leave the relationship at this point, to cut and run.

Part of the problem at this stage is our unwillingness to reveal who we really are. As Colin Caffell, therapist and workshop leader, says in *Facing the Fire:*

> As a society we have a tremendous fear of truly expressing ourselves from the heart. We fear what might happen if we let our true feelings be seen – no matter how justifiable. We believe that to express them might mean some form of destruction or abandonment, even insanity. But then the alternatives are not much better: depression and self-pity, powerlessness, bitterness and resentment, to name but a few.[7]

There is destruction here, but it is not what we think. Caffell is right, but as yet it might be cold comfort. A fight is a fight, after all. And something is dying.

A fight is about intense frustration as well as anger and behind it there is the fear of being powerless. Fight, with its opposite of flight, is always about fear, disguised ... but it is usually *also* about a desire to connect more deeply, consciously or not, to reach and be reached. Fighting happens when our loved one seems to go beyond our reach. So what *is* really happening here?

Our wounded histories are emerging, side by side. We are putting the masks of the past over each other's faces where before we had put our best hopes and light. We can imagine this almost like theatre, the lovers literally masking each other. In reality, *we don't see ourselves doing this.* And what we cannot see controls us, it runs the show. That can be the most destructive thing of all. What we do see is still the face of the man or woman we love, but the feeling has changed. *They* have changed. Apparently.

This is where the work begins. Because we have to learn to ask, listen and see. We have to go behind each other's masks and ask. Where have you come from? Why am I feeling like this?

Our story continues:

*He had a mother who was physically unavailable. He had no breast-feeding and too little actual contact. He was left alone crying. He can remember this and the rage he felt at not being met. This is what he is looking to heal.*

*She in her turn had a mother who engulfed her with attention, because her husband left her. Although he later returned, the memory remains. Of course, there is anger that her father left as well as uncertainty about her place in his affections.*

*His need for contact, which is like an ache all over his body when she is near or when he feels desire, becomes transferred onto their sexual relationship. But when she feels this, she feels engulfed and as if she has no choice – and so she withdraws.*

*She becomes his mother and he becomes her mother. Both of them feel angry. Neither of them are getting want they want.*

Our childhood wounds, carried in our stomach area (the solar plexus), are all about *wanting*. What we actually *need* is something else. For now, we have conflict and blame. This is the movement back and forth of transferred pain. And because our egos and our sense of pride are involved, the pain is compounded.

*He feels rejected as a man. She feels used as a woman – as if all she is there for is to ease his aching. And because she can also do this, he wants it!*

This is what is happening as they lie side by side apart in bed. Their wounds are both evoked and seemingly exacerbated.

At the same time, their anger conceals their fear. Both share the experience of being abandoned – she by her father, he by his mother's later death – and they are both scared that one of them is going to pull the plug and vanish into the night.

This is but one of the many instances where we can hurt each other because we are not getting what we want, as well as regressing to our most primitive responses, which are to scream for what we want, as we once did...

## Deconstruction

The closer we get to the roots of our stories, the more energy there is, but also the more pain. This is the direction and downward movement of the *nigredo*. It takes us to our roots, underneath the self we have constructed to compensate for our inadequacies as well as to survive. But because this self (or 'false self' as Hendrix among others calls it) cannot be all we are, it is basically a shield and an armour. It is a constricted, defensive version of ourselves. And the irritating thing is that it acts like an automaton. It is our own little Frankenstein of survival and sometimes – perhaps all too often – we can't switch the damn thing off.

Nor is there only our defender to reckon with. There are all the lost and repressed or disowned parts of ourselves which we will also see in our partner and be attracted to *and repulsed by* . Why ? Because we have not owned, or re-owned them in ourselves. All of these need naming and clarifying as well. Her 'judge', and his 'seducer'. Her little perfectionist and his Peter Pan. They are all present and they all emerge in the longer phase of deconstruction that *nigredo* and subsequent stages of the process go into. They are part of the many and different strands that are being separated out as part of the fact of our difference. In our sameness that we merge in, we cannot see them.

So, for now, the journey is to the root of pain – and the root of love as well. *Because it is love which is doing this.* This is terribly important to grasp. Love leads us within, to our core scenario which holds the greatest pain and the greatest energy. It is like an acorn of fire and it is where our untransformed pain and anger burn. We are separated from this hot deep place in order to survive – it would be like permanent torture or hell-fire otherwise. But we are also separated from it *by our minds*, which tend to to move away from the very thing we need to engage. *Nigredo* here is very much about the mind, and the death of the mind in a certain sense. During this stage we move, or are moved, *from the head downwards*. We are moved into our feelings and our body. So from darkness we come into the fire.

We can experience this for instance in the difference between cold and warm anger. Cold anger is like a razor blade, it is of the mind. Warm anger is from much lower down. Both are seeking relationship, but with cold anger relationship is impossible, for it is simultaneously fear of anger, and it repels us, it pushes us away. Warm anger, on the other hand, is seeking to connect. Warm anger signals that the core energy is moving.

*Because of her core pain she is seeking above all to be met in her anger. She knows this is what will make the difference. He is also needing to be met and needing to be believed in as a man.*

*This challenges her to stop projecting her father onto him. At the same time he is challenged to control his inner child's wanting.*

And both things are still going on. The fight continues.

*She flings off the ring he has given her. It tinkles somewhere invisibly, never to be seen again.*

And they both have to burn before a thorough deepening can occur that is inclusive of both of them.

No one has put it better than the late nineteenth-century French poet Arthur Rimbaud:

The fire within you
Soft silken embers
Is our whole duty –
But no one remembers[8]

His second line is important here. Warm fire already carries the vein of healing in it.

And there is water here, anticipating the next stage, because now we have two wounded children who are both crying, as well as two adults who are grieving the loss of what they have shared, even as they may dimly perceive a higher purpose behind it all.

Of course there are moments of clarity, too, that remind us that what connects us is still very much alive alongside all the unfolding complexity.

*She sees him briefly, fleetingly, without any mask, as he is, and for the man she believes him to be – and he sees her in what she needs, with an aureole of space around her, and within it, her whole pelvic region expanding, opening and flowering, her womanhood blossoming in roseate fire.*

*And in a calmer, bluer light, new possibilities dawn like seeds, like a New Year's morning when the slate of the page is wiped clean, and they both see what their love-making could be, beyond the paralysis of antici-pated sexual moves and responses, when instead there is no agenda, only the moment by moment presence of feeling and intuitive touch, experimenting, listening in skin, and trusting.*

Then, after a brief respite, the fire will come back again, deepening in its spiral, and we see what it means to be with another in the absence of love.

How can we be with all this emotion and reactiveness? *Being* is the key as we approach the root of one another's woundedness, where possibly no one has trodden before. Even as we may recognize what the issue is and where it comes from, this is where analysis alone doesn't work and where trying to 'fix it' doesn't work either. Here we must simply *be*, and in the present, sitting in hell as the depths of lovelessness show themselves, as the wounds we have suffered are revealed. These base parts are what Sri Aurobindo called the 'primary mineral controls'. In alchemy they are seen as the deepest part of the *materia* – the 'stuff' that we bring to the alchemical flask to be slowly transformed.

This process is especially powerful where any form of abuse is concerned, particularly sexual abuse, which leaves a residue of wanting to expel everything that has invaded the body, as well as the potential of deep self-hatred and possibly self-harm. All these things will remain unhealed as long as we are unwilling to open to them. That takes courage. But nowhere is lonelier or more frozen than our deepest places of pain.

*And so he sits crosslegged on the floor with her, holding both her hands as she rants. Later the self-inflicted black bruise on her thigh is the mark that shows she has been here, where the central knot has been tied.*

What does it mean to *be* with anger or rage, when it's the last place we'd rather be? Again, *being* is the key word here. To suppress the rage is useless – it makes a real meeting between passionate adults impossible – but equally to act it out is likely to be as humiliating as it is distorted, as well as terrifying for our most vulnerable parts. Again, there is a third point here, beyond denial or reaction, which is *presence* - being in the presence of each other that allows another quality of attention to be present - and this the thinking mind alone cannot accomplish. This quality of presence is what allows compassion to manifest, for our partner - and ourselves.It also allows emotion to transmute into feeling - into what is *behind* the emotion and *within* it, as grief (for example) is behind anger.This softening is also what brings us from the solar plexus into feeling and the heart, as we will see.

\* \* \* \* \*

So in learning here what love is not, it is humbling to realize *how unloving we are*. That is what brings us to our knees. The gap between our thoughts and our actions, our words and our deeds becomes increasingly obvious in this *nigredo* darkness which has a light all of its own.

> *He makes a list, and on it includes the following:*
> - *his insensitivity towards her, for all his apparent feeling*
> - *his pushing her with what is actually his own need (and not hers or 'theirs')*
> - *his superiority, his fear of emotion, his reactiveness and pride*
> - *his fear of what she might do, and his defensive mental ego.*
>
> *She makes her own, as part of a ritual they are doing to draw a line, identifying what they want to let go of as well as the qualities they want to take on.*
> *There is a quietness in the room at last, as the candle flickers...*

And since the word 'trust' is also on her list, we might ask how can a woman trust a man until she has shown him her worst? This is where she renounces carrying his *anima* – his archetypal feminine – for him in order to assert the reality (and pain) of who she is.

And he? He also needs to be who he is, so that she can accept the fundamental need to connect with her own sense of spirit which she has projected onto him. He needs that from her.

It is important to 'be for real', as Leonard Cohen has sung. And we're all going to be 'hurt by love', as he suggests, but actually it isn't love that hurts us, it's we that hurt each other by not being true. So what dies in *nigredo* is also illusion, and perhaps a certain false charm, a niceness that reveals itself as an unwillingness to engage with what is really going on, wanting peace instead at any price. The price is likely to be the relationship sooner or later !

Instead what we have here is something rather different. What we find at the heart of the *nigredo* (because the darkness has a heart too) is a longing for transmutation. We long to be able to show ourselves to another as we are, to acknowledge our dark side and have it received: it is one of the most difficult things we can do. In the ancient world, in Greece for instance, a man would have been received sexually by one of the temple virgins (*virgin* originally meant 'a woman at one with herself', not a celibate) in a rite known as the *hieros gamos*. This was no ordinary prostitution. He would be received by woman *as he was*. Later, he would have to leave the enclosure and go on his way.

We can see the secret at the heart of things here: *that love draws all that is loveless to itself, and that is why love goes to hell..*

It may have to go more than once too. There is much to transmute. The work has only just begun.

## The Residue

After all this, what we are left with is what alchemy calls the ash residue, which is what remains at the bottom of the flask after its contents have been blackened and burnt. It is referred to as the soul. It is tenuous, but it is there, where the fighting has died.

What is left now of our relationship? Exhausted as we may feel, something has been freed. It may be too early to say what. Do we even still have a relationship? That is for each of us to answer individually. Certainly the relationship will need restating and we may be unable to do that as yet. What is left is the ash – and the need above all to go beyond emotion and to *feel*.Otherwise we might as well be dead.

\* \* \* \* \*

This, then, is the fruit of *nigredo*. It gives us another way of looking at hell or the netherworld – as a place where we see each other as we are, while realizing who we are individually at the same time. It reveals the reality of a relationship as a vessel for healing and transmutation (what we secretly want), without in any way diminishing our deepest feelings, our desire and our passion. All of these are needed here. Most of all it involves a willingness, in love, to be with the absence of love, for this is what love draws to itself. In so doing, we are broken down by love into a deeper potential for loving.

'*I accept you as you are.*' Can we say this? And still hold our hearts open? And can we keep owning the difficult things in any moment, in any of our relationships? Then we will have begun to tame the raven of *nigredo* and to see that it is another face of the dove.

The questions and exercises that follow in this and subsequent chapters are suggested to help you locate your own awareness and also to ground your own insights in dialogue with one another. You may do this work with a current partner or internally with a previous partner or spouse you are separated from. You may also do these exercises if you are on your own in relationship to yourself.

Either way, I suggest you stay within agreed time boundaries and aim not to exceed an hour for any exercise or combination of exercises. It is important both alchemically and emotionally that the work is contained in this way, also that it should take place in a conducive environment (perhaps not in a public place, for instance). I also recommend you stretch, move around and/or go for a walk afterwards and that you 'close down' if you have been doing the meditation exercises. You can do this simply by visualizing the energy centre of each chakra from the crown downwards to brow, throat, heart, solar plexus, sacral and root as a flower that is closing, then surrounded in light. You may find it useful to have a notebook or journal to hand overall, and also to be aware of your dreams as a result of doing this kind of work, because of what is stirred in the unconscious.

Finally, if you don't already have access to good therapy or counselling, whether individual or couples, it may be useful for you to consider this as another container and mirror for this demanding journey that you are making in and through love.

### Coniunctio

**Context:** falling in love/returning to love
**Key question:** what is the vision of your relationship ? What might this love serve?

The flask, in other words, *the container* is vital for the alchemical process; and every relationship needs and benefits from a sense of containment.

**Try this:** I want to suggest you begin by visualizing two containers. The first is for yourself, the second is for your relationship. See the second surrounding both of you. In both cases, notice its quality, its colour and texture.

Then, with both, taking one at a time, reflect on what its gift is to you - what it is trying to show you. Ask yourself 'what is it trying to show and give me ?' And when you have a sense of that, ask it what *it* needs from you.

Consider then what you need to make your relationship a sacred space.

Whether you do this exercise together or apart you will of course both see different images for your relationship flask. So take some time having clearly seen your own  to compare notes with your partner.

First, share your individual images and discuss what they both represent in terms of your own sense of containment and relationship with yourself.

And then place the images of your relationship flask side by side and reflect on what they are both holding or representing as part of a larger circle that is more than both of you individually.

## Nigredo

**Context:** Death of ego, freeing of soul

**Key question** (alone, and with your partner): What are you being, or what have you been brought down to?

### In looking at crisis and descent together:

Consider your projections on your partner, on how you see her or him. Who does she or her remind you of from your history/your family ?

Consider your anger with your partner.How might you be looking to your partner to heal the wounds of the past? What are these wounds – where do they come from?

What fears do you evoke in each other – can you name them? What is it like to be able to name your fears ?

### Attraction/repulsion/control:

What are you attracted to and repelled by in your partner?

How far can you relate these aspects to things you haven't admitted or owned in yourself?

How do you seek to control your partner ?

**Overall:**

If you have idealized your partner, can you see how you might now be devaluing her (or him) ?

Consider the difference between relating to your partner from an emotional place - and from feeling (the heart). What is the difference for you ? How do you experience it ?

These are questions to hold, and discuss. You may also find it useful to write about them before sharing.

**Try this:** consciously bring the focus of your attention from your head into your heart. Begin to experience your partner from your heart. Notice how this changes what you have been thinking about her/him.

**Try this:** Sitting with a lighted candle, let your partner speak strictly without interruption for five minutes. Pause then for a minute or so, before you respond for the next five minutes. If the atmosphere between you has been bad, you also agree not to leave the room and not to engage in any form of physical coercion.

**Try this:** Sit in silence with your partner for 10 minutes. with your eyes closed, holding the affirmation 'Wanting you to be who you are, I accept you as you are.' Be aware of what happens in your thoughts and feelings, including any resistance, without trying to change it. Stay with it.

**Try this ritual:** Make a list of things you want to let go of from your behaviour in your relationship. Write them out in a list and then tear them into individual strips. Sit together with a lighted candle (or fire) and, consciously naming each aspect aloud, let it go into the flame/fire. Watch it/them burn.

Gather the ash afterwards in an envelope. Seal the envelope. You may choose to keep your ashes or dispose of them, perhaps treating them as parts of you that have died.

## Chapter Two

# Heartwork

*solutio* – purification
'the relationship we dream of'

Blood must flow, he said
For the garden to flower;
And the heart that loves me
Is a wound without a shield.

– Jalaluddin Rumi
trans. Andrew Harvey

A shower of rain, falling suddenly out of nowhere, streams in the visible air, filling the space of your eyes as you gaze out at it ... leaving you listening to the sounds of it running into the gutter, or dripping off leaves.

\* \* \* \* \*

*He drives into the thick of the city traffic, leaving her still in bed behind him, as a sadness begins to settle like a soft weight around his heart. 'How much can we bear to feel our feelings?' he wonders.*

\* \* \* \* \*

The sickle moon, high in the sky, like a drawn bow, or a boat breasting the clouds that scud grey around it as the stars prick out one by one. And everywhere, it is as if something is trying to link up...

\* \* \* \* \*

We are surrounded by images of feeling, but that doesn't mean we feel. Often we are unconsciously fighting *not* to feel. It is as if we have a basic fear of being engulfed or 'drowned', of losing control, of losing ourselves. Experiencing the flow of life in our feelings should come naturally to us, but all too often we hold ourselves tightly in, dividing up our lives in watertight compartments. The price we pay for this is exile and disconnection. So we discover something basic: *that to feel outwardly and to feel inwardly are indissolubly connected.* We cannot do one without the other.

And why should we feel? It is simple: because we cannot love otherwise. Feeling, and the softening it releases, is what brings us back to our hearts.

### Solutio

The challenge to live a life of feeling is at the heart of this next stage, which alchemy calls *solutio* –literally, 'solution'. We can think of this in both the liquid sense and in the sense of solving a problem or resolving an issue. Difficulty can be hard and unyielding, solution often is not. We may be surprised by softness and by how tunnel-wide our view in retrospect has been.

This links to the core alchemical dictum, which is *solve et coagula,* literally meaning 'dissolve and re-form', or 'die and be reborn'. This is what alchemy invites us to do. We have already seen this in *nigredo,* where the ego loses its prominence and the Old King loses his throne. *Solutio* continues this work in every way and we need to see these two stages as two sides of the same coin, rather as the black and white of the yin/yang symbol are to be found in each other, their colours separated only by a fluid wavy line.

Here in *solutio* the colour is white, with all that white suggests (purity, cleansing, clarity), but it is also a white that shines in the dark with a lustre like pearl, silver-white, like the moon. The two planets associated astrologically here are Jupiter—the opposite of Saturn—signifying expansion, and the moon, in all its phases from dark to full. With the moon we have the feminine, specifically Luna herself. She holds the key.

The Dark Night of *nigredo* has freed the soul. Now it has been loosened, the soul itself needs to be worked on so that we can recover our capacity for feeling and receptivity. This is the logic of this next stage. At the same time, as we enter the realm of feelings, we discover that our feelings are far from pure. They are not only blocked but full of static, as well as being changeable, irrational and unclear. But when feelings, or we might say *emotions*, are first freed, that is how they are: *nigredo* reveals them humiliatingly as a can of worms.

## Separation

What prevents us from feeling, what separates us from it? Separation is where we begin, and in another sense of the word, which alchemy specifically calls *separatio*. This means that having been together we need for a time to move apart. There is a transition, an almost imperceptible movement... as in the whitening of a winter dawn. We have to come *back to ourselves* to allow an integration of what we have experienced in coming together, and for this, separation is essential. It allows us to see ourselves, as well as each other, more clearly. This is a basic rhythm in relationship that can be effected in different ways, whether we live literally apart or together. It is a rhythm and a need, and it asks to be honoured. We cannot feel and be receptive to this third body between us otherwise.

Here we also begin to do something that is vital in the work of love. We begin to see the one we love as *inside us as well as outside us*, finding each other in our own hearts, not just outwardly through our eyes. But there may be distortions here.

45

Separation can also create conflict and polarity. Harville Hendrix describes this on an emotional level in terms of 'fusers' and 'isolaters'. Fusers want to get closer, isolaters want to get further apart. And each holds the shadow, the opposite, of and for the other. Fusers are out of touch with their need to be separate. Isolaters are out of touch with their need to be intimate. In most relationships, one or other takes either part – and in different relationships we can play different parts. We are not simply typecast in one role.

This suggests something revealing: which is that every relationship has its natural point of balance or equilibrium, measured invisibly as with a spirit level, which it will always be seeking to return to. This is a both-and state that encompasses both closeness and distance, heat and coolness.

But because we bring our unresolved needs from the past to relationship, that level, with its ease and calm, is easily disturbed and can get lost. As we say, we 'lose the plot'. It may look as if one or other of us knows how to be in relationship; the reality may be *that neither of us does.* And this is painful to recognize.

*His separation from himself is in his adoration and fixation. At moments, he just can't take his eyes off her. As they walk down the cobbled street, he looks at her in spite of himself like an adoring boy. This irritates her. She knows instinctively that this spells mother – and need.*

*She meanwhile has her own separation issue. Hers is from her own body and, as a result, her own feelings – and so also from the man she is walking with. And her frustration with herself can be easily put out onto him, as he reaches for her arm...*

It is here that the separating out of emotional content becomes particular and necessary. We see what is activated between us whenever we connect—and then separate out what belongs to *you*, and what belongs to *me*. It is only when this outward process

46

is made conscious that we have the opportunity to turn our own awareness more deeply inwards. Intimacy (which means to 'meet within') is, after all, also about our relationship with ourselves. We can see this in terms of energy: without this contact, or capacity to relate to ourselves, *we are pulling at the other to complete us*, to fill the hole we feel in us; and we can do this literally, or in the way we perceive and manipulate the other ('Be Daddy – get me out of this hole!'). And this is what the wounded child-like parts of ourselves will invariably be doing, which is why we need to understand each other's stories before the story that we share can really make a difference.

## Luna

*Separatio* is what happens naturally at this stage in our story – later, it is more conscious and can be more freely chosen. For now, it also has to do with Luna coming into her own empowerment, both as a woman and as the feminine principle. This is because it is her qualities of listening, receiving and communicating that are vital here – and at the same time, more magically or mysteriously, it is she who brings a different aspect of consciousness that is integral to the whole work of opening up to feeling.

We can call this 'soul', as it is fashionable to do, but this can be too limiting. The traditional distinction of the feminine as simply *soul* and the masculine *spirit* is a half-truth which actually furthers the division between men and women in subtle and unhelpful ways. She is soul *and* spirit, as he is, and as alchemy itself insists. What we can say is that soul is more obvious here at the beginning of this stage and spirit is more manifest at its end. But it is essentially the feminine, and the otherness of the feminine, that is revealed and exalted here.

Luna personifies a consciousness that the patriarchal world has downgraded and denied. She is the lunar side of consciousness, reflecting the sun in her dazzling white mirror as well as changing in her phases. She is also 'lunatic': mad, dispossessed, out of reach of solar reason. And she has two sides. As Llewelyn Vaughan-Lee writes:

> The feminine is both creative and destructive, nurtures life yet also devours it. The *anima* has her dark side. She is the siren who lures men into the waters of the psyche and leaves them to drown. Belonging to the impersonal depths, she is cold and uncaring; she seeks only for power and uses all her magical attraction to imprison consciousness.[1]

There are women who do this, especially in the movies. But we need to be careful here not to confuse the archetypal with the personal, and in so doing muddle a negative male view with woman (any woman) as she is, in all her moods. Above all, she is fluid; in alchemy, quicksilver as opposed to sulphur, which is Sol's more fixed and constant mode.

Esther Harding gives us a valuable clue, in commenting on how women are ruled by the lunar cycle:

> For woman, life itself is cyclic. The life force ebbs and flows in her actual experience, not only in nightly and daily rhythm as it does for a man, but also in moon cycles, quarter phase, half phase, full moon, decline, and so round to dark moon...[2]

And she adds:

> When a woman at the dark of the moon is disturbed by a sense of disharmony in herself, iritability, inertia, or restlessness, she may be able, by deliberately taking time alone, to gain a unity of psychological aim within herself...[3]

The phrase 'unity of psychological aim' is suggestive of who

Luna is and how she functions. There is a quality in the feminine which deconstructs the masculine, not simply for reasons of revenge, spiteful criticism or power, but because it is *her* penetrating quality that alone can reflect his awareness back to himself, changed. Otherwise he cannot see what it is that he is doing. And this reflection may well include reflecting back his *anima* (his feminine soul) to him and refusing to carry it for him because it is exactly what he needs to get in relationship with for himself, as well as because *she* wants above all to be seen as she is, and not merely as a screen for him.

At the same time, those negative shadow elements can be present – the shadow itself has two sides (positive and negative). In the unconscious woman, these are not differentiated: she is not aware of which she is in and what she is doing with herself. She is changeable (as the moon is); she can be tricky, cold, controlling, narcissistic and manipulative. She can be every bit as disconnected as any man. Conversely, there are men who are more in touch with their own feminine than some women are: more sensitive, and less self-centred, too.

Luna is *all* of this, in so far as she is All Women. In alchemy, as well as being her human self, she is muse and initiatrix, and she is Sol's awakener to feeling and heart – and ultimately to the man he is. She is (as Vaughan-Lee adds) 'the messenger of meaning',[4] bringing a message that takes place through dissolution and feeling without which neither she nor Sol could realize their spiritual potential, either alone or together. Her key is sublimation: meaning a raising up of energy, which includes sexual energy.

In archetypal terms, Luna leads Sol like a horse to water. She dissolves him and the dry concepts of his thinking. She brings a moistness to his ideas about life and relationship – she brings him soul. And through the expression of her innate qualities *she also purifies herself,* including her own shadow, contacting her own need to feel and nurture herself as woman, to be *more* of a woman.

So, in *solutio* the *materia* —our stuff in the flask—is purified, in fact 'whitened through to the bone' in a repeated dissolving, evaporating and recongealing that we can think of as laundry in a washing-machine cycle, as the temperature slowly rises. That is what is going on in the alchemical flask and in the relationship at this point – and it brings us more closely to look at feeling.

## Feeling

An image that often appears in alchemical illustrations at this stage is of the pelican piercing its own breast to feed its young. This gave rise to the 'double pelican' (see Introduction) symbolizing our couple linked in the work. Alchemy sees this as an expression of what it means to contact and open the heart. It is painful, and it must be done. 'Blood must flow...' as Rumi noted. This flow is the flow of feeling for which blood is the metaphor.

What is happening here in a word is *heartwork*. And heartwork is very different from head work, not least because most of us don't know how to do it. We don't know how because the mind of the heart is not the intellectual mind, with its tendency to fixed emotional responses or reactions. The heart-mind is spontaneous, immediate, changeable, as fluid as molten wax. It skids, slides, reverses and progresses in a continuous present of overlapping threads, rather as a conversation does. It is closer to poetry than prose. Nor does it simply use words. It is closer to the senses and more at home there.

Because of the plethora of feelings evoked at this stage – in the water – the initial experience is of instability, contradiction, of mixed messages even; of anger, fear, insecurity, of love and power combined. Sol especially is likely to be confused here and Luna's messages may well not be clear. He may feel he is being asked to stand on his head at the same time as standing on his feet, but that is perhaps because she is more at home with confusion than he is, and for her, two contrary things *can* be true at the same time.

*Two, or more than two even! 'Share your feelings – but don't react to me.' 'I want to be met – but not with anger.' 'Ring me when you want to – but give me space.' 'Love me – but don't* make *love to me.' He wonders at their extent.*

Maddening as these mixed messages appear to be, they can strike him sideways like a series of Zen koans. What *is* the sound of one hand clapping? And the point is, we can't 'get it with our minds', but in the pause, something else can arise, which is awareness. As psychotherapist Sohani Hayhurst put it, memorably:

> The way of the heart is not easy,
> The way of the heart is not reason.[5]

And through the awareness, a purer response can come, which is feeling... rather than reaction or riposte. And Luna is ready for that – *that is what she wants.*

*He cries at her leaving, simple vulnerable tears. She puts her arm round him. She cries with him. But as soon as he says 'Don't leave me,' she flinches. It strikes off key. And he knows it.*

Nor it is all one way, even as she is taking the lead. As he responds in feeling, this reflects feeling and a greater sense of clarity to her. The seed of a truer, deeper communication is born between them, centred in the heart. She in turn speaks of a clear core of feeling emerging in her, around which there is, however, still stuff to be worked through, the accumulation of habitual and conditioned responses from her own control system. She knows it.

As John Welwood suggests, vitally at this point:

It seems that the only way to move through the disappointments of relationships without harming ourselves and others is to actually open the heart *more* at the very moments we would most like to close it off.[6]

With that clarity we can see that here in the whitening we are *feeling what is loveless and what separates us from love.* It is in everything we say and do when feeling, and respect for the other's feeling, is absent. Without feeling, if we look closely and honestly, there will be another agenda. It may be manipulation or veiled emotional threat. It may be simply mechanical, like a pretence. But its effect will be the same. It will not bring us closer.

So we can begin to see what is being washed and cleansed, and we can begin to appreciate the meaning of 'dross' (another word that derives from our framework here). Dross is everything we do that needs to be made transparent, so that we can see what we are doing and be aware of our impact on each other.

At the same time, we need to allow ourselves to make mistakes. Speaking from the heart is not a perfectionist thing – on the contrary, it can bear any number of crossings out! The important thing is *to allow ourselves to speak*, recognizing that if we repress the heart by trying to be good, or saying what we believe the other will want to hear, the heart simply 'backs up' with unexpressed feeling that can make matters worse. This again is where we have to trust, risking our vulnerability all over again...

Sol drinks the water, as he knows he must. If he is wise (or foolish enough) he will let it run all over him and he will put his head under it as well !

*He rings her back spontaneously to acknowledge what he was also feeling, but not saying. She is moved and the message she gets is that he can face his feelings. As a result, she feels closer to him. They can go further.*

*She can allow him to touch her in a way that feels right, where she doesn't feel invaded or forced to respond. He discovers to his delight that this is more intimate than he could have imagined, or than his erection could have told him it would be. He can be with her as she is, feelingly, letting her (for now) take the lead; even inviting her to, without repressing his own desire.*

*And she in turn, like the soul sister she also is, will lead him to the pure place of feeling where there are no words, there is only touch, gesture and breath – the fullness of her lips and the precise moment of caress as he listens to his hand touching her skin.*

We trust feelings here precisely when we let go of needing to speak. Feeling, that is heart-centred, is the key. Then, even if difficulty continues, clarity can be there too – we can 'see' what is happening where previously there was only conflict and confusion. In this we can appreciate the difference between emotion and feeling, where emotion, belonging to the solar plexus, is reactive; and feeling, which belongs to the heart, is always receptive and responsive.[7]

As we grow in feeling and the freedom it brings, the issues between us are shrunken by right perspective. We can see this literally with our eyes. We become aware of light *around* the things we are seeing, just as the third body surrounds *us*. The function of the third body is part of this same energy at a higher rate of vibration, just as feelings themselves *are a refined and evolved state of emotion*. Feelings take us beyond our learned responses from history into the more generous and gracious realm of the heart. And it is in feeling that the soul comes alive in its true fire. As feeling emerges, though, we may also need more space than before, especially if we are in a situation (outwardly or inwardly or both) of constriction. Newness needs expansion, as flowers do to open.

*He knows he is a man daring to live his heart and to inhabit its*

*physical skin in a way he never has before. He knows that this is her gift
to him, because she is here, even as she comes and goes in herself.*

*He knows it like a fine rain, inaudibly present, gathering to fall
behind his eyes as he thinks of an absent friend, of the woman he left, all
winter on her own in grief, of his own father, frail with his old blood like
wine, and as the sense of it gradually spreads, encompassing the sheer
fragility and limitation of life, the rain falls, and he knows what it
means to be in the Land of Tears, and how love's way only comes when
we open our hands...*

## Sex

There is another way of looking at the issue of sexuality here that
is central to what this stage is about. Sex as we have known it is
largely based on emotion and ego. It is more or less a blind
projection of our own desire, or our mutual lust, if they happen
to coincide. Sex like this is the physical expression of uncons-
ciousness, though it has its place as well as its pleasure. But as the
*only* form of expression it is regressive and its language jolts and
betrays itself accordingly: *'I just want to fuck you'.'*

Because sex has been so repressed as part of our collective
shadow, we have had to suffer it in an untransformed state. But
to then refuse to look further than its Cunt and Tits shadow is to
misunderstand its whole purpose and to betray the heart of our
physical being. D. H. Lawrence knew this long before permissi-
veness:

> The subtle streaming of desire is beyond the control of the
> ego. The ego says: 'This is *my* love, to do what I like with! This
> is *my* desire, given to me for my own pleasure!'
> But the ego deceives itself.[8]

Alchemy has known this for centuries. Part of the work of feeling
in *solutio* is about the transmutation of sex itself.

This is deeply connected to the feminine and the receptive – as opposed to the blindly penetrating masculine, the one-eyed Cyclops that wants its own way and its own satisfaction. Of course a woman can want this too, in her own way, insofar as she has learnt to be negatively masculine, to have balanced the scales only in terms of power, not love. But perhaps we have to know the 'zipless fuck' before we can know love. Then again, perhaps we have to relinquish it, too. But one thing is clear: sex won't be caged. Like anything, it can only change if there is freedom to change rather than coercion. Sex has its ego, as we have seen. Confronting that ego head on only strengthens its hands-off reaction – and understandably, because for many of us it is the only free, or seemingly free, place there is.

We need to know there is another place and we may only find this when our sexual ego breaks down, our performance breaks down or when our body says, 'I can't do this like this anymore.' In *solutio*, that is what Luna, the feminine, says. She says, 'No.' She may say it emotionally or she may say it physically, through candida, thrush or bacterial vaginiosis, but either way, she says it. For the moment, it is no.

What dies with our sexual ego, as well as the pretence, and the attempt to please, is the perception of ourselves and the other *as an object rather than a subject*. In that objectified seeing, we don't have to *feel* the other, we can simply desire or lust after him or her. As soon as we start really feeling for the other as a person, or as soon as the other comes or dares to come close enough, we can't do this anymore. But what also breaks down is a form of control, which is what seeing someone else as an object also is. And, like the heart, this is what needs to break ... or open.

So, for a new sexuality to come into being for Sol and Luna, or any of us, there will probably have to be a period of celibacy and withdrawal, and fundamentally (on both sides) the feeling of having a choice about it.

In *solutio*, Luna withdraws. It is not simply for herself,

whether Sol knows it or not. It is also part of his initiation. She withdraws sexually to reach the root of her feelings and the wound that separates her from being able to feel and be open to him as well. This is not morality. Nor is it tameness. It is actually about wildness, the true wildness that only comes when we have contact with ourselves, contained – and therefore at times restrained – in who we are.

As Clarissa Pinkola Estes puts it, in *Women Who Run with the Wolves:*

Many women fear natural celibacy. It is a period of purification in which old habits of relating are purged. It is a period in which a woman is finding new roots for relationship within the security of her own feminine grounding.[9]

And, as she goes on to say:

If the morality of the body demands a temporary cessation of sexual activity, it is not a period to be feared. It is a phase: the fuller relationship will come.[10]

This is alchemy and out of it something new as well as 'the fuller relationship' can come. Again, feeling holds the key here, because what does come is a sexuality that is grounded in sensuality and the body as it is rather than what we make it or force it to do. What comes is *receptive* sex, deep sex if you like, that Tantra, with all its similarities to alchemy, has also known for centuries.

Tantra is an excellent critique of Western sexuality. Tantric practitioners speak of 'the valley' as opposed to 'the peak' or 'summit', in extending the time we make love. Here the valley means letting go, going *down* in this sense rather than going up. For men, it witholds orgasm so that the energy of desire can rise into the heart, and so into feeling. This changes our experience of sex completely and it doesn't require a handbook of strenuous and dramatic positions either. It simply means relaxing where we would normally only experience tension: letting go, breathing out and being open to what is there moment by moment and touch by touch. It means being *in* touch – inhabiting our touch, really dwelling in it, as we do in our hands and fingers, and staying in touch. It is the opposite of what we have known. Through it, we can move from harder to softer, more soulful sex, and it is there we will find Mercurius again, radiant and awake, showing us that the third body is also our sexual as well as sensual body with all its freshness, spontaneity and playfulness. But first the old way has to fall into dissolution.

*He feels it as they lie together in the morning, with a space between their naked skins. It is the image of a man that he has also partly contributed to, interposed like a skein or film betweeen them, which makes her fearful and makes her anticipate: what he will do if she leads him on, what she must do if she is to please him. This is the antithesis of her freedom.*

And actually, his as well. We can say that what is needed here is also clean communication. We need to tell each other what we are feeling, and what we feel like and *don't* feel like sexually, recognizing also that it can change. This is fragile as well as fertile ground and it can easily be trampled. So it needs tending. And patience. Flexibility – and space.

### Power

And of course the shadow of all of this is present too. How could it not be? So we find ourselves in a power struggle. What has been broken open emotionally in *nigredo* continues here and the quest, through the water and then the fire of this stage, is to find its resolution. But the power struggle is also a process in itself, not simply a static series of self-repeating events, and it is important to see this. We can be changed by the struggle – *if we engage with it in feeling and not just in our minds.*

Essentially the power struggle clarifies itself here. The surface friction reveals the issue beneath, which we may not have been initially aware of. What are we really arguing about here? As Harville Hendrix says:

> Once a relationship seems secure, a psychological switch is triggered deep in the old brain that activates all the latent infantile wishes. It is as if the wounded child within takes over.[11]

As he goes on to say, revealingly:

> This gave you the sickening realization that not only were you not going to get your needs met, but your partner was destined to wound you in the very same way you were wounded in childhood![12]

This reveals the power struggle for what it essentially is: as a struggle between two wounded children with a root fear of annihilation ('If I don't get my needs met, I will die'). We love each other *and yet we are fighting for our lives.* Furthermore, we are not simply two children here, we are also two adults living in a difficult and imperfect world which doesn't by any means necessarily meet our needs or respect our feelings. It is painful to have that world intervene when we have known a very different kind of world between us. It's here that the shadow of our loving is revealed in all the moves for position we make. Why? Because just as the relationship can raise us up, so it can also – seemingly – dash us down and leave us without hope.

The power struggle in this sense is a suspension of the third point at the apex of the triangle that is the spirit, and grace, so that the two points that mark the lovers at its base can *really* change.

*She longs to be seen as she is, not just as beautiful like an empty frame. She longs for space and to be able to feel. Now all she can experience is this wanting to push away. At the same time, this is her own rejection of feeling and of something she knows is challenging her to the core.*

*He longs for her to come closer, not to keep breaking off and moving away. He longs for a continuity of loving between them. Why does she have to keep breaking it off? At the same time, he is pressuring her with what he sees and not acknowledging the needs he can only meet in himself.*

Neither will give in. Neither feels they can give in. And although there are lulls, moments, even days when what is between them lifts back to lightness, expanse and rightness, the struggle comes back again like bad weather neither of them can control.

What we need to do here is see behind the mask, understanding more about each other's behaviour and what it is covering; and not just in terms of core childhood issues. We have to include our various adult parts – our subpersonalities or variations of self – as well. What is it about you that needs to be superior? What do you achieve by making me feel insecure? Or, to take a concrete example, the seducer's need to be loved and not to be abandoned results in: 'I will abandon you before you abandon me.'

So it is not only our wounded childhood that controls us emotionally, but also our *adulthood* we need to look at here. In practical terms we have to look at what Michael Gurian calls 'the control system', meaning how we try to control each other in service of our own needs. This has to do with our personal boundaries, and our energy. It also has to do with our defences. With love, we come forward in the circle of who we are; with power, the current is reversed - and we withdraw. When we fail to get our needs met, or respected, we create an exaggerated behaviour where those needs become over-emphasized. We can both behave artificially in this sense, whether we are fusing or isolating. It is important to see this in energetic terms and also important to see that *we are both right*. It is only then that what separates us can begin to reunite us, when we have suffered our own limited view and really seen the other as he or she is.

This means vulnerability, which is what is required here. This is the opportunity. But in the power struggle we are *not* - by definition - willing to be vulnerable and are stimulated by the negative images we conjure of each other in our heads. These make us even more unreceptive to who we both actually are. It is as if each of us passes through a distorting filter. We can no longer see the wood (let alone the trees) for frustration.

*They polarize respectively. He becomes fire in a rash of feeling. She becomes ice and can feel nothing.*

It is like a fever. How can it break? When it reaches its contained limit, when the energy itself and its heat has done its work within us.

The only obvious outcome of all this, apart from the couple's separation, is for us to become not only adult, but also free, to stand within the circle of ourselves, to become (as Gurian says) 'a self that is not dependent on another for its spiritual centering'.[13] We have to find power *in* ourselves, as opposed to reacting to the other – or even by perversely finding it that way.

A triangular model from Gestalt psychology illustrates this neatly. At one side of the base we have VICTIM. At the other, PERSECUTOR. At the apex, we have RESCUER. We can can move between these three positions in relationship to each other endlessly. However, the only way out of the triangle is ADULT. This opens the ground for a new kind of relating where we are free to respond. This, however, remains closed as long as we refuse to face ourselves alone in the strangeness and pain of our solitude.

Our solitude may be more an avoidance of relationship than a rooting in who we truly are. This is where it is important to recognize that boundaries, for better or worse, are also about defence. Are they still serving us? That is the question.

## Fire and Water

We also need to ask ourselves what is being born at this point of apparent *impasse,* in this insoluble space? Difference and clarification, certainly, that prevent merging – even as we long to be 'as one'. Alchemically speaking, within both a woman and a man, both Luna and Sol, we may find that what is being born is *her fire and his water.*

This stage begins in water and what it moves towards is fire. The sense of being softened, of being in the unknown and of losing our usual grip may last for some time, but clarity does begin to come as our eyes adjust in this very different realm that remains essentially Luna's, where Sol, for the moment, is eclipsed. The movement here in consciousness is reflected in the emphasis in this stage on dreams – we will tend to dream more here, and being awake to our dreams and their suggestions will lead us on. Reality itself may also be dream-like. It is fluid, as we are.

*Solutio* is about movement, because that is what feeling brings us to, and this includes the experience of being stuck, as we have seen. Alchemy would say that generates the necessary energy if we can stay with it, and always in alchemy we are advised to embrace two things: *patience* and *trust the process.* Psychology knows this; alchemy embodies it.

Power can either be a struggle or a momentum that carries us forward. It may have to be both before the momentum can be revealed and what separates us from it becomes clearer. We need to be adult, but we can be *too adult* as well. We need to use our minds, but we can end up in our heads getting nowhere. This is what *solution* in all senses, in its wisdom and foolishness, can teach us. This is also what Mercurius will show us – if we give him or her half a chance.

Alchemy offers us a way of seeing that addresses our fundamental dilemmas in terms of energy – in terms we could say not only of mind, but of feelings and body at the same time. Alchemy's belief is that whatever is there is there for a good reason, otherwise it wouldn't exist. This gives us another way of looking at 'solving', grounding it in acceptance (as well as restraint) within the agreed safety zone of our own alchemical flask, that is our container and our sacred space.

Within it, everything between us is activated, everything is moving to make the *materia* golden. We are not in sight of gold as yet, but we could say that here we are panning for it in the river and finding specks of it in those moments of gleaming insight that come.

A particular kind of seventeenth-century laboratory flask was known as the pelican. Another version of it was the double pelican I have mentioned. This is really how we need to see Sol and Luna, Luna and Sol, at this time. The two flasks are side by side and joined together as the *materia* circulates between them. It is an intimate reminder of the reality of transmutation between two people, especially when things are at their toughest.

If water and fire describe the process of solution, then their interaction describes what happens at an energetic level between Sol and Luna, masculine and feminine. First, in the water, we may have to visit our own soggy foundations, our origins as human beings, alone and perhaps together; but then, as more feeling is freed and the heat rises, we discover a fire that can burn in the water, a liquid fire. We can think of fire as activity here, as well as heat, and water as receptivity. Or we may think of them as yang and yin, but also as metaphors for feeling in every sense these two words *fire* and *water* convey. And as Sol and Luna interact (in or out of actual love-making, or wherever they may be in between), *her need is to be fire, his to be water.* This is where she takes the lead. She contacts her strength while he strengthens his capacity for feeling. In terms of their gender, *she becomes more feminine through her male energy, while he becomes more masculine through his female energy.*

Then they can dance, as the air between them moves.

*And as they do, he sees her eyes so vivid blue under the blonde highlit curtain of her moving hair, meeting his, and he knows he cannot hold or control her. She is herself, as she always will be.*

*And as he looks for a moment into the room full of swaying undulating figures, all in a free fluid form of their own, he suddenly sees life like water in his hands, something that he can't hold either, but only cherish and let go, being a part of it, surrendering to it.*

In this dancing, we can learn to really *be* in the present moment of feeling and we can dance our awkwardness, dance our pain, dance our hesitation ... and as we do, so it can change. We can dance together then as we are, with faith and without expectation.

*She tells him, 'When you let go, I can breathe. If you hold on, I hold myself rigidly.'*

*'It's not about leaving you,' she adds, 'it's about moving.'*

Moving – so we may see that our essence is freedom. We may remember here also the rigid couple we saw in the last chapter and how their demise can finally come when one of them softens or is softened – perhaps by circumstances beyond their control. Through freedom and movement, as Francesco Alberoni states:

...falling in love continues because the nascent state is reborn over and over, in a constant revision, rediscovery, renewal, self-renewal, a constant search for challenges and opportunities. Then we fall in love again with the same person.[14]

How can we sustain this? In a phrase, by staying in touch. Losing touch is losing trust, too, and losing trust feeds losing touch. Then we get stuck again in a power struggle of the mind. Yet, if we wait for it to grace us, *solutio* can dissolve the impasse and the feelings can flow free...

## Awakening

As feeling opens, *we reach spirit and spirit can reach us*. This is not a disembodied state, it is an extremely subtle and sensual experience *in* the body, just as making love is. We can experience it in our blood as well as inside our skin, as energy rising. We may even literally feel hotter for no obvious reason. The purification of *solutio* is also described as 'the spiritualization of the body'. In fact both these two stages taken together, forming what is called 'the Lesser Work', perform that function. This means we can feel things in a way we may not have felt them before. Our watery nature, with its molecules filled with space, becomes revealed as a vessel that energy oscillates within and constantly passes through. We are like doors left open to the wind. We are much more physically spiritual than we know.

Alchemy's vision of heart opening and its blossoming here is described as the *Rosa Alba* (White Rose), a flower of love – a love that is achieved through the purification of emotion and romance. Just as the whiteness here is extracted by repeated washing from the lead and depression of *nigredo,* so we could say that the love is extracted from our initial falling *in* love. It is also, as we have seen, a love that has been through the fire.

Then we may find that our *conuinctio* beginning returns to us, reappearing through the descent and the purification of *nigredo* and *solutio,* and that it is the love beyond projection that is pure seeing, seeing our lover as he or she truly is.

Now we move into *sublimatio* ('sublimation'), the final part of this stage, which includes a second *coniunctio*, or coming together, of our man and woman which is very different from the sex of *nigredo*. Alchemy pictures Luna with Sol underneath her, making love to him as he receives her. They are also pictured in the form of an androgyne, as woman and man, man and woman together *in one body* as an expression of the blending through fire and water that has taken place, and of the body that is between them. There is a sense too in which they are literally reborn here, tempered in tenderness, open to healing, where the barrier between inner and outer has been dissolved.

This is a time of vision for them then, a time of gifts given freely. It is like their first time, but now there is more awareness, not only of each other but intuitively as well. There is a knowing in and through the things they see and feel which is perhaps more direct. It is certainly less emotional, less clouded by that heady rush of champagne sunlight. It is a different taste, closer to the purest mountain water, almost unbelievably soft in the mouth.

*She walks alone in the gardens, delighting silently in the spring crocuses, variegated white and mauve and wet with rain.*

*As she tells him, he feels it. He imagines her there, where they will soon be walking together.*

There is a knowing, too, because of what they have suffered. They know more of love because they know more about the lack of love. They know each moment is precious. When our hearts are open we may think simply of the one who is walking beside us as a transient being whom we will never see in this earthly form again.

We can look at our fears about intimacy and realize that the relationship between us is *ours to create*. It doesn't have to be a certain way. Again this is different from the first meeting, when shoulds and oughts are more obviously present. Remove the pressure of what you're supposed to do and how you're supposed to be and what do you find ? The freedom to make it up as you go along. Something is glinting in the watery sunlight...

*As they walk down to the ponds, twin large circles of water separated by a sandy path that intersects them at their centre, they notice the swans. At first glance, there to the right, just beyond the cawing black ravens, among the ducks and the coots, a pair of them are in the water, and then in front of them too, as they turn, another pair, one in each circle...*

*And as they walk ahead, they enter an extraordinary silence where the dip of the land shields them from the park roads and the city beyond, as the birds sing minutely in the spring air, and they can hear each other breathe. Past the lightning-blasted oak with its black hollowed trunk and collapsed arms, they turn to the right, wandering among the oaks with their age and strength, as he wonders, wanting to ask her for a tryst. Not a ring now, or even a binding promise – what could it be? Something out of the air that marks this, that says 'Yes' to it, that says, 'I want this life with you.'*

*As they emerge onto the open grass with some white towerblocks rising beyond, even as an ambulance siren wails through, they are still held as if in an envelope of silence, like a letter opened inside-out held in a hand, as they trace a broad arc back at last to the other pond's side.*

*And as they stand there, the picture forms in front of them: a couple walking slowly around the pond's rim, in black; and a man, all in white, in green Wellington boots with his golden retriever. The couple passes them. They are young, hesitant, wondering which way to go. The man follows, middle-aged and grounded.*

*Then they are left looking into the water as the sun begins to set among the clouds beyond, slanting its reflection among the ripples where the swans drift, until the water softly blazes like glass as they gaze, incandescent, and one of the swans, drifting closer, turns blue in*

*the reflection as the water becomes a quivering electric dance, wholly
sentient, like a message that is wordlessly and perfectly itself.*

What does 'perfect' mean? Alchemy says it means 'complete',
'accomplished', and yet more real than any picture or made-up
story, like the two glasses of red wine that appear on the table
between them by the unlit white candle at an empty restaurant
table for two. Could it be this simple?

## The White Stone

What we are left with here is the white stone, which is the end
point or punctuation of the work so far. As with all things in
alchemy, it is both literal and metaphorical, literal as the purified
material which results from repeated distillation and coagulation, and metaphorical because its substance is also *a quality
inside us.*

The white stone is where matter meets spirit. It is said to have
been pulverized until all the blackness has gone from it,
indicating a thorough purification on every level of mind, feeling
and body. Alchemists have seen it as Christ.

And the white stone is more than this. As one alchemist has
written, it is 'the white sun, the full moon, the fruitful white
earth, cleansed and calcined [cleaned by fire]'.[15] Others have
spoken of 'matter elevated to the lunar state'[16] reflected in our
ability to see with the heart's eyes, as well as sensing the invisible
permeating the visible, the way a sea mist creeps in...

And in us? We can think of it as clarity, forming like a crystal,
and as a cleanness on every level of our being. It is also the
strength that clarity brings. It is the ability to hold spiritual
energy without becoming inflated, self-preoccupied or 'too good
for this world'. It is also about our values, what we believe in and
live for. At the same time it gives us an openness to another
world, a lightning-like intuition, so we are 'in the world but not

of it', as St John's Gospel has it. We can be 'Higher than the World'[17] in this sense; we can get a clearer view.

The white stone in us is a refinement of the process from water to fire, and one indication that we have it is that we don't regress into the more shadowy aspects of the water we have passed through, which are narcissistic and addiction-oriented, pointing towards unreality. *Solutio* can be a womb we can get stuck in, just as *nigredo* can be a repetitive self-negating nihilistic trough.

The white stone gathers the threads of the soul it clarifies, of the separation and reunion of the purity of the feminine, of the heart it opens and liberates from emotion, of the power it releases in energy, of movement that it reveals as freedom, and finally of the love it brings in an awakened heart. This reveals its quality, finally, as *the power to love*.

\* \* \* \* \*

Some alchemists stopped here and some relationships do, too, going straight into marriage. We, however, have further to go. We are called deeper again and outward too – into the greater world that is also a greater love.

## Solutio

**Context:** Purification of the soul, true romance

**Key question:** (alone and together) What is your relationship to feeling? What does it mean for you to open your heart?

How much space do you give to sharing feelings, your experiences and your dreams with your partner ?

Try making a commitment to doing this for an agreed time each day where you can both be relatively relaxed and receptive, morning or evening.

**You may also consider:**

What is your relationship to water? What may need to be cleansed or purified between you?

**In terms of *separatio* (separation):**

Consider the space and time you both need individually so as to be able to come together creatively and give of your best tyo each other. Where is the optimum point of balance between being together and apart for you?

**Sex:**

What do you feel about sex and what do you expect of your

partner?

How might your sexual expression change in terms of being more in tune with your partner?

**Control (and see *nigredo*):**

How do you seek to control your partner ?

Try this: in a private room, both of you stand and assume your positions of control and demand in relationship to each other. Gesture this physically. Notice what your gestures are. Then each of you explore your partner's gesture instead, and feel what *that* is like. What do you notice ?

Discuss together.

**And in finding yourself at this stage of the process:**

Try reflecting or meditating on the following key words, taking one at a time, perhaps over a five-day/working week period:

- control
- containment
- surrender
- openness
- trust

Be aware of any resistance that is evoked as well as awareness and insight that comes. You may also wish to share this.

**Try this:** Sit quietly, and again take a moment to connect to your own heart, then imagine connecting to your partner's heart. Notice what it is like to feel this bond between your hearts. Can you?

**Try this:** Sit again facing each other without speaking. Just make eye contact for two to three minutes. You may need to look away then bring your eyes back. Be aware of what and who you are seeing.

Then make contact with your partner's hands. Close your eyes and be aware of what you're feeling. Allow your hands to move together and be still.

Then, releasing your hands, see if you can connect to a third point (like the apex of a triangle) above and then around you. Then connect to the sense of presence between you, really letting yourself feel it.

**Try this:** sitting quietly, connect to your heart, breathing into your heart chakra—just above your sternum—for about 30 seconds. Then bring your awareness to your crown chakra on top of your head, and breathe gently into its area for a further 30 seconds. Then bring your awareness back to your heart chakra, and rest there.

Reflect on what it means to come back into being 'in' love.

Reflect on the power of love, and your power to love.

# Part Two

# The Greater Work: Coagulatio

Facing forward
with our eyes open –

out of the deepest and most natural
home of our seeing –

we stand in the moment
shaped by living hands,

and cross the threshold
of this river
into the realm
of the Greater Love.

Chapter Three

# The Desert Journey

*coagulatio* – grounding
Venus
'the relationship we fear and resist'

Where a man's wound is, that's where his genius will be.
– Mircea Eliade

Imagine you are walking in a field. The field is so long you can't see to the end of it. You look down at the ground and see that it is bumpy and uneven, made up of tussocks of grass and clods of impacted earth as well as stones. You need to look ahead, to raise your eyes to the skyline, but you also have to look down—or else you'll miss your footing.

## Coagulatio

This is *coagulatio,* and taking the word *coagula* (literally meaning 'coagulate', or 'thicken and congeal') after the *solve* of the last chapter, it means coming down and coming to ground. This is new ground, new earth as opposed to the old earth of *nigredo.* And new ground, by definition, has to be 'broken'.

The story of alchemy is full of unexpected twists and turns, which, as Johannes Fabricius rightly says, 'compel the adept to ever new adjustments, unexplored procedures, unknown attitudes'.[1] That is worth remembering here, for it is part of the drama that these changes and shifts all happen quite naturally, even though their logic escapes the mind. They point instead to a deeper rhythm and sequence in the psyche or, to be more precise, the *mind-body*, which is why alchemy is such a deep and enduring frame of reference. As people have said to me when I have been teaching the subject or including references to it in therapy, 'You know, this is exactly the kind of thing that has been happening to me – it's just that I haven't realized it.'

After the whitening of *solutio*, there is nowhere higher to go but into premature disembodiment. We have to come down. We have to let go of the white stone, to let it fall to the ground. Something larger here in its challenge, unique to alchemy as opposed to many religions, is the bringing together of spirit and matter. That is 'the Greater Work', which takes place both inside and outside us.

*Coagulatio* brings us to the threshold of the Greater Work and to a grounding that is vital to the achievement of the whole work and the legendary Philosopher's Stone. After the spiritualization of the body, which is the goal of the Lesser Work, there is now the *embodiment of spirit*, which also means a facing outward into life. It also means bringing spirit into life and therefore form. This is alchemy's vision. It is a vision in which we live beyond ourselves, becoming connected - in Dante's phrase - with 'the sun, the moon and all the other stars'. It is a vast exploration of union, which is why it is called the Greater Work.

## Core Gender

What does this mean for our lovers? Where do they now find themselves? As Francesco Alberoni says:

> The relationship between falling in love and love itself, between nascent state and institution, is comparable to that between taking off or flying and landing, between being in the sky above the clouds and firmly setting foot on the ground again.[2]

This links us to something that is of particular importance in the work of this stage that we could simply call 'core gender', meaning who we deeply are in our masculine and feminine being. It is an unearthing and differentiating of what really makes us men and women beyond the usual stereotyping. It is not enough here for each of us to be an undifferentiated mulch of masculine and feminine – that is not going to take us further. Instead it is holding an awareness of both these energies inside us *and* getting to really know our own man and woman. This includes being aware of what also attracts us to members of our own sex, confronting us with our *own* gender and with all that may be repressed there in terms of our experience. This is vital both to a grounding and deepening of who we are in our physical being, whether we are literally 'gay' or not. This is what lies at the heart of Sol and Luna's journey now and it is what takes them beyond being prince and princess, or *puer* and *puella,*(boy and girl) and into the deepened dimension of king and queen.

And it is what makes alchemy what it has always been called, 'the royal art', stretching us higher and deeper than we have known into what is innate in all of us.

*They arrive at the summit where the landscape opens out to the rolling fields and hills beyond. The spring sun blazes clear over their heads, with the grass fresh and new under their feet. Then they start walking down to what appears to be the Ordnance Survey point, marked with what looks like a giant birdbath. Only as they approach do they see what is on top of it, rising in metallic coppery green like the emerging earth, with gold shining through its worn engraving – a 3D land map of where they are, pitted with paths and ridges, boundary lines and names. She pauses, looking down at it, smoothing its edges with her hand. Then they start walking down towards the open fields below.*

*Near the bottom, the path narrows. They veer right from sunlight into the shadows of the trees and the cloying muddy ground. A heaviness slowly comes over both of them in the silence.*

*Then the path ends and they are left on a sloping edge among fallen branches and last year's leaves, trying to find a way through. At last they come to where a wire fence runs and they lift it carefully for each other to crawl under.*

*Walking on, they can see exactly where the shadow meets the sun, ahead over the grass, like a borderline. They step back over it with a smile and begin to slowly climb the hillside with its warmth on their skin...*

*Then they are lying back with the afternoon sun shining down on them, his shirt pulled up and her white soft stomach exposed, after looking down over the curve of the fields in the luminous green-gold light and back towards where they have come as they share a final orange, resting replete, feeling the warm earth under them, their eyes closed as each reaches for the other's hand...*

That is the journey of *coagulatio*, with its descent and its rising, its difficulty and eventual temporary repose. It is a journey that comes from the element of earth itself – from the ground itself and what living on the earth means, from the clay from which our lovers are made, with all that it calls them to become.

Its colour is yellow, like the sun, and associated also with intellect, creative energy and the will. These are all qualities of the masculine; in contrast to *solutio*, where the emphasis is on Luna, the focus and spotlight now is on Sol.

The yellowing is also connected to the stone, for it is what happens to it here, in preparation for becoming the Philosopher's Stone. The white stone is yellowed by its own ferment, by being earthed, in other words, 'little by little', as it is said, and this gradual nature points to this stage as being the longest of all. It is the stage we mostly find ourselves in and returning to in different ways. There is a weight here, a gravity which draws us back, that also has to do with the soul as well as earthly work and duration. It is part of our commitment to the Earth and being 'of the Earth' that also translates outwards into green awareness and responsibility.

\* \* \* \* \*

There are two parts to this stage, which come from its association with two major and more personal planets – Venus and Mars, which also signify the archetypal feminine and masculine energies here. They stand like gateways that our lovers pass through. *In Men are from Mars, Women are from Venus* John Gray speaks of them memorably as polarized places which need to become more aware of each other's language. In alchemy, the added dimension is that *we each contain the other* – a woman *also* has her Mars, while a man, as importantly, has his Venus. Their contrasexual development at this stage relies on this, in the sense of who they can both become.

## Sol

Separation here is the natural end of love-making. We come together, then we move apart. It is the opposite of struggle – and it is at this moment that Sol begins to sink into the element of earth, to fall into himself, into an experience of everything he has been avoiding by 'going out of himself' to her. This is where a man finds inner pain, emptiness and feelings of inadequacy, and at the same time, in letting go of Luna as an individual woman, he is opening to an expanded and more archetypal feminine all around him that is Venus. This is where he needs to learn to feed himself directly and inwardly rather than being dependent on an outer woman. This is especially acute for men who have had insufficient mothering and who will otherwise constantly look to their partners for what they never had and in a sense never *can* have until they embrace the feminine *as the earth* as well as within.

This is where the work of differentiation begins that is Sol's initiation into himself.

## The Desert Journey

I call this 'the desert journey'. It is a very contemporary journey for increasing numbers of people. For a man, *it is a journey where he has to take on what a woman holds for him in and through himself.* This happens elementally in terms both of his earth and – because he is thrown back on himself – also his fire. These two elements belong to Venus and Mars and their associated metals, copper and iron respectively, where copper is soft and pliable and iron is fixed and strong. The desert journey, which is also very much Luna's, or woman's, as well - where she has to take on what a man holds for her - involves a differentiation which leads both of them into themselves in terms of their own connection to the source, however we understand that, whether as the Self or Oneness, Christ or Buddha. We cannot say *what* it is. We may simply call it 'essence'. The important thing is that it is something we can experience and that it is connected to our physical being.

We have seen this already in terms of the third body that two lovers make between them. Now we each have to find that feeling quality *in and through ourselves,* which is essential to having a spiritual life beyond dependency. This is also the gold, which begins to appear here.

The desert journey has a quality of limbo about it which resists our controlling and coercion. It has its own timing which connects us to where we are right now – and which may also involve saying something that the other doesn't want to hear. At the heart of it is the mystery of the inner marriage, the fruit of the relationship we have with ourselves that makes an outer or actual wedding a different reality. That is what its journey reveals.

Embarking, we leave behind romantic love as we have known it, stepping out into something more difficult and yet miraculous.

79

## Venus

The stages associated with Venus are:

*fermentatio*
*illuminatio*
*nutrimentum*

In all of these, Mercurius, who is as much connected in alchemy to the instinctual as he/she is to the spiritual, appears in the form of a snake who slides into the flask and winds round the 'philosophic egg' (the work so far), squeezing and penetrating its shell as it cracks open. We can understand this 'cracking open' as a breaking of the existing wholeness so that a greater wholeness can come into being. In this sense, Sol is being deconstructed by the feminine again, but this time by Venus – the archetypal feminine quality that also relates to the earth itself, rather than just by Luna as an individual woman.

*And by himself, too,* by what he comes into in each of these subsequent mini-stages:

## Fermentatio (fermentation)

In *fermentatio,* Sol is opened to his essential male energy. We can think of the process of fermentation (with beer, for instance, or leaven in dough), which is also one of agitation. It is here, as the whiteness begins to be yellowed by the action of sulphur, that alchemy associates Sol *with his own semen.* This is his essential energy and power as a man and it is out of this energy that he is formed, not only in terms of conception, but throughout his life. He is now turned back to his core energy at a physical level, having previously had his focus more exclusively on Luna and her allure.

The agitation here is not so much about arousal as awareness, then. Sol's semen is also about his potency –his perception, his discerning, his mental energy – and at the same time it is about his fertility as a person. This is also something literal. Alchemy does not like to see our minds and bodies divorced from each other.

So this is what Sol is immersed in, as is Luna, too, in terms of her inner male and her contact with that energy inside herself.

## Illuminatio (illumination)

From this comes *illuminatio*, in which the gold – unstable and coarse as it initially is, as 'green-gold' – is said to appear. *Illuminatio* is about light and it is also about awakening. The sun's piercing rays may awaken a man to himself here, often through criticism, or a 'reality check', which is where Luna may also literally come in, giving him unpleasant feedback. If it is accurate, it is likely to 'prick' him. We all know the feeling and we'd rather turn away. Because *illuminatio* is about our blind spots, it can be deflating, but insofar as a man can open to it he can as a result *begin to become his own light,* and this is the purpose of this part of his descent.

## Nutrimentum (nourishment)

And there is further to go. The last part of this work under Venus is all about nurturing and nourishment. It is the *self-nurturing* that a man receives when he begins to connect with his own feminine through Venus, and not as anima but as nourishment, literally feeding from the earth as we do every time we eat what the earth gives us. This is *nutrimentum,* through which a man finds his own 'heart of earth', his green awareness. In this sense too a man becomes renewed. Another word for this stage is *cibatio,* which means 'feeding the new'. An earth mother is shown holding a baby and in a way this is also Sol, because the experience is likely to evoke his own infancy and he is a child of earth in this sense as well.

Men are softened by the earth, but they often battle against this softening because it evokes an unsettling vulnerability. It is likely to reflect a man's relationship with his mother, feelings which may be unconsciously re-enacted with each woman he is with. There is a certain helplessness here as well. This may even be physical, if for instance our experience of this stage has to do with illness, even temporarily with a bout of 'flu, where recovery takes its own time. But we have to experience this softness, or alchemical 'copper', otherwise the iron we move on to in the Mars stage will not be truly strong but as brittle as it is unfeeling.

## Descending

What is the guiding thread through these stages of descent? For both our lovers, on this part of the journey separation is again relevant – but it is a separation that is about preparing for a different level of connection. And in this process the couple's actual separation may be the outcome. This is because we do not yet know who we may become. We may have to let go of our ideas about ourselves and our relationship.

Letting fall the white stone doesn't mean abandoning ideals and principles, but recognizing that they have to come to earth, just as an idea (this book) has to in order to be a reality. Yet as an idea enters form, a sense of loss and disappointment is often involved, which is why we sometimes prefer to keep ideas 'up in the air' beyond the clouds so they will never be spoiled and never die or fail. But then life will remain more of a dream than something actually lived. Disillusionment can also enter here with the realization that our partner is as imperfect as we are and cannot provide all we might wish.

Letting go of the white stone also means entering into an *expanded* realm in the sense that reality is always more than our limited perceptions of it. This expansion is not simply about our potency in a relationship, or its shadow, control, but a *spiritual* power in and through which we can be more of ourselves, as we now need to be.

So the first movement of this stage is a turning into ourselves. Finding we cannot go further in the form of *solutio* with our partner, instead we have to return to our own self and ground. In concrete terms, we may have to live alone, for however long we may need to.

## The Beloved

Within this solitude, when we don't try to escape it, something can come that otherwise could not: *our relationship with the source of love that is invisible, that is the Beloved.* However we understand or experience Him or Her as teacher, guru, goddess or guide, by definition the Beloved is in a place of *greater love* and so is our doorway – however small, however improbable – into a greater loving. So we begin to be freed from wrongly seeing our partner as the source of all love. This is a step we all have to take.

At first it is lonely. It is empty, just as a container has to be empty before it can be filled. *But we have to make space for the Beloved* or, as often as not, that space is created for us, sometimes through painful separation.

But then what comes into our hearts and beings is an awareness that we are spiritual beings within our skins, connected as much to what we can't see as to what our eyes can reflect. And we may also find, as Rumi did, that 'God, too, desires us.'[3] Not only this, but we need to feel desire for God, just as we do in any relationship with a man or woman. We need to find our own way of relating to Him/Her, because our relationship needs to be individual and personal. This contact may come through writing as well as drawing and painting, as it has for many artists who find themselves portraying something larger than life, whether consciously or not.

Then a revelation is experienced – *the Beloved talks back*. The Beloved can and does come right into our innermost hearts. To receive this enlightenment we have to be still, just as we are when we sit in meditation and let go to that which is greater than ourselves. Stillness is the medium of transparency, where the walls of the physical world go thin and where we can allow in what is beyond, what John Welwood calls 'the mysterious power and wisdom of the universe', 'the Beloved we most long to join with'.[4]

At this point we are also likely to experience what separates us from it: our fear of losing control, invasion and surrender, and of not being able to have our own will. What we later discover is that *the will of the Beloved and our own are actually the same* – it is only we who have been resisting who we are, what we feel and what we need.

It is important to remember that, as Welwood also says:

Only when we are devoted to realizing our own true nature, with the intensity and passion we usually reserve for romantic pursuits, will we find the ultimate fulfilment we seek.[5]

However, this process can go alongside relationship if we are wise – or perhaps simply graced. As a friend said to me, 'If I can remember the person I love is a reflection of *all* I love, I won't get so consumed...'[6]

When we realize we are in relationship with someone *who must also have their own relationship to love,* we have opened this door to the greater loving and the Greater Work. And then, perhaps instead of 'ultimate fulfilment', what we have is the journey, a greater love we can live, which, I believe, is our deepest longing.

At the same time, we open the door to uncertainty as well as grace and freedom. We cannot have freedom *and* a set of guarantees, much as we would like them. This is an issue which is basic to this stage, where disillusionment can mean being let down and even betrayed. Sometimes we can only come to ourselves or back to ourselves when we *are* 'let down', and then the ground we have to stand on is also paradoxically made of uncertainty, just as solid ground is also made of particles of moving space.

But this is the uncertainty we need if the fullness of love is to be...

## Passion and Release

This is where we are brought to – and to a question that can rack us inwardly with its contradiction: how do we relate to the other fully and passionately, while at the same time be willing to let him or her go?

First, we can only love like this by making the relationship we have with ourselves *permanent,* not as a selfish or narcissistic preoccupation, but as solid ground that is going to be there all our lives, no matter what. This permanence is another step in the inner marrying, an aspect of the stone which is strengthened by this coagulating process.

Secondly, we have to love the other *in the present,* here and now as he or she is and not maybe or later. That is another aspect of this descent.

Loving the other in freedom also means surrendering to the mystery that is the third body between us, and increasingly we find that is revealed in a palpable rather than abstract way and, in intuitive flashes that may surprise us, we *can* understand each other. This is where a greater loving also comes in, because it also requires an attitude of mind that is part of this 'body' of intelligent and sensual light between us.

Every time we surrender in this way we take a step further into the desert in the direction of soul and spirit rather than ego.

## The Mystery of Desire

Sol's descent under Venus begins with desire – where else but in the place of his greatest need after food, warmth and shelter, the place from which he is inexorably drawn to the other? As well as contacting and visiting a more ancient part of ourselves, which our sexuality carries from the primordial past, we also need to ask in the present: what makes me needy and dependent sexually on the other? This in turn relates to a deeper question: what is it we desire in each other? What do we want?

We have to go to our individual experience to answer these questions – there can't be a generalized response. But what follows are some of the issues that Sol, or any man, faces at this point.

The first has to do with *merging*, where a man still wants or needs to feel like a child, consciously or not, and 'at one' with the woman he is with, either because of an absence of mothering or because mothering was not a safe space. If incest or any other kind of abuse has been involved, a man's need for a good mother will also be tinged with anger, fear or loathing and may express itself in a complex charade of attraction and withdrawal which hurts a woman every time. A man has to be thrown back on himself to see what the pattern is here - and it is certainly desert work. You can taste the sand in your mouth.

A second area, which may be related, involves a man either being sexually aggressive or – at the other end of the spectrum – passively not owning his sexual fire. These may seem poles apart, and in one sense clearly are, but a man who is not in touch with his sexual fire may seek to control his partner's response in subtle ways so as to avoid contacting a deeper, more expressive and surrendered part of himself. While this can also be true of a woman, one of the greatest gifts a woman can give a man is the chance to let this deep part of himself be realized.

A third issue is where a man cannot love himself sexually and is dependent on another person to do so for him. This may or may not involve actually masturbating, which may or may not be pleasurable or effective, but the principle remains. Steve Biddulph suggests:

> Self-pleasuring – for both men and women – is a kind of apprenticeship. It's an important source of self-awareness – a prerequisite to being good in bed. It's here we learn what we like, so that we can communicate this to our partner. It's here that we learn to let ourselves be totally receptive (a difficult thing for many men) – surrendering, allowing one's whole body to receive the loving energy that becomes freely available in sexual exchange.[7]

A man's willingness to love himself and honour his own sexual needs takes tremendous pressure off a woman. The important thing is that he can say: *'I have a sexual relationship with myself ,with or without her.'* He may even need to say it as an affirmation before it can become a reality.

The fourth area relates to the second, which involves a man's capacity for containment. This isn't simply as graphic as premature ejaculation (though it may involve that), but has to do with his ability to *hold* his own sexual fire as well as *feel* it. Again, this isn't just so a woman has time to be physically ready to receive him but because sensitivity also requires restraint, a pausing, a waiting even, otherwise his lack of containment can make her feel overwhelmed emotionally, as if she has no breathing space. Passion can trample and lead to a person feeling simply used, which will undermine the ground of feeling between two people.

And fifth, especially relevant for heterosexual men, is our relationship to our repressed homosexuality, which many of us still don't want to hear about. This is a key to feeling closer to ourselves *as* men – and to the feminine either in another man or in ourselves. This inner contact changes our relationship to ourselves, making us more relaxed, sensual, present and embodied.

This relates finally to an area that men perhaps find hardest to own and that is: *our attraction to a woman comes from ourselves and not simply from her.* As Steve Biddulph asserts:

> In seeing women as the holders of sexual attraction – as having power over men's desire – men actually *give away* their own sexual energy. We put women on a pedestal and then resent them for being there.[8]

This is where it is worth examining our sexual history to see what our personal issues of power and attraction are.

Again, this is complex. Love of the feminine can involve giving our power away until we realize, perhaps years later, than a more real love involves holding on to that power. This is also related to the issue of being attracted to more than one woman or how when a woman doesn't respond as we want her to, our attention 'goes elsewhere'. Infidelity may also mean that we are incapable of being faithful to *ourselves.*

It can be humbling to realize this, but it brings us down to our own earth. Humbling comes from *humus,* which is 'of the earth'. It also brings us to the deeper question of our relationship to the masculine in terms of our fathers.

## Fathers and Sons

In alchemy, who would Sol's father be? He isn't named as such (nor is Luna's) and he isn't the Old King of *nigredo,* though in some illustrations a king's son is shown with his father and there is an uncanny resemblance between them. In a sense this lack of naming shows that fathers often represent what sons have avoided looking at. Fathers often hold the shadow, which actually can be a thankless task.

The way a son feels about his father will have its origin in his experience of him as a child. By the time a boy is adolescent his trajectory will often be *away* from his father into an attempt to become *of his own* making – and it is here that his flesh and blood feelings can become buried. If a son's orientation is then more towards the company of women, men as a species can easily become somewhat distant and unknown to him.

And the father himself can be distant, absent either literally or emotionally. As Robert Bly points out:

> The father is remote: he's not in the house where we are, he's somewhere else. He might as well be in Australia.[9]

I first read these words with a jolt, because it was exactly where my father was at the time!

When the father is absent, it is into that void that demons may come and the father may become the shadow, even a representative of the collective shadow: all that is dubious, materialistic and degraded, like gold turned to excrement – the dross, in other words. As a result, the son – as Sol, his name is oddly significant here – *often seeks to redeem the father by transcending him,* just as Icarus in the myth flies above his grounded father Daedalus until the wax on his wings melts and he comes crashing down into the sea. Sol is a *puer* (eternal boy) here in a classic sense, reaching for the light above the perceived darkness of his father. However, as Bly states:

> Flying of that sort does not *rescue* the father either. The ascensionist son is flying away from the father, not toward him. The son, by ascending into the light ... to some extent redeems the father's name.[10]

But at some point the trajectory is (as the Icarus myth demonstrates) reversed and the son falls to earth. This may come initially through the astrological Saturn Return (first occuring between the ages of 28 and 31), which is often associated with *nigredo*, but will appear increasingly with the process of age as a man goes from his thirties into his forties. He is getting closer to the earth, whether he likes it or not.

It is here that a man's relationship with his father stands to be renegotiated, and perhaps seen for real, beyond projection, for the first time. It is here that a man discovers a deeper bond and realizes that he needs his father *as the first man in his life.* Father here becomes the source from which he receives a particular transmission and substance, a 'male milk' that is emotionally connected to the experience of his deepest energy – again (as alchemy sees it), his semen. There is a mystical bond between father and son that is vital to a man's feeling of having a foundation and place in the world.

Many young men tackle their absent fathers through exterior structures like college or the police, taunting authority to get a response they so desperately need and a boundary they have never been given, yet institutions cannot substitute for the real bond. A father's absence will leave Sol with an absence of substance as well as constancy, like the alchemical flask and its contents, which of course affects his relationship with any woman. At some point there must be a rediscovery of and return to the father, whether he is still alive or not.

The closing of the gap is a gradual process which can take years. These are some of the issues involved.

First is a son's recognition that he has more of his father in him than he has recognized or been willing to admit. I remember vividly the moment which ushered this in for me. I was in my mid-twenties when Carole, my partner at the time, remarked, as I was reversing the car into a space, that I looked exactly like my father. It came as a shock but also a strangely welcome surprise. Something in me began to feel warm. Steve Biddulph expresses it well:

> Your masculinity – unconsciously and whether you like it or not – is based on his. Most men realize (with alarm) that their father's mannerisms, stances and even words are deeply a part of them and likely to emerge at any time. If you are at war with him in your head, you are at war with masculinity itself.[11]

The second issue is a son's awareness of his father as an individual human being as well as 'his shadow'; and this involves being aware of his father's life, of what his choices and struggles have been, and what he has carried or is carrying as a result. A father's story is vital to a son, for he passes on the substance of it, as a distillation, to him. Even if the son never gets to hear the father's story as fully as he would like to, he will either become conscious of it (if he can) or it will haunt him. It is here that the son goes beyond being a child or a 'boy-man' in wondering, in wanting and needing to know, or know more. It is here that he can begin to really see his father as he is and connect his experience with his own sense of being a man.

I will never forget standing at my father's eightieth birthday gathering and hearing one of his oldest surviving friends describing his bravery in the dark night of the North African campaign in World War II, 50 years before. Suddenly, in a quiet, cracked voice, he was describing in graphic detail my father killing enemy German soldiers silently in the dark with a kukri knife. The room hung silent. Here was my father, this ageing, frail, kindly man, and here was I, suddenly aware that what he had done was a part of where I had come from, part of my own inheritance, part of the determination that flows in my own blood, even though I shall never fight in a war of that kind. Suddenly I saw all I had avoided – and I saw my own battle and the source of its strength.

The third area where resolution and a real healing can come is when we recognize that a father also needs his son's respect and that he will wait and go on waiting for it even to the end. For this, a son has first to be aware of what his father's gift is to him. This requires that he go through the wounding that separates them and then makes the return journey, either with the father himself (preferably) or with the surviving relatives.

At the same time, a son has needs too. He also needs his father's respect to complete the circle of their relationship. That respect frees a son to not only feel a oneness with his father, but also to go on his own way towards being the individual he is, rather than remaining in the guise of an ageing rebel, a reactive rather than affirmative spirit.

I and the father need to be one on Earth as well as in heaven – and that can only be achieved when we can say 'I love him.' It's then, perhaps, that we can really find our feet.

## The Child in Time

One of life's mysteries is how we have to 'go through' our parents again and again to become more of who we are. They stand in front of us like gateways, as they did when we were born, and our passage through them is vital to our own lives. Denying them is denying our earthly being, even though at the same time we come as independent souls from our own heaven and with our own journey. Working with our parents *inside* ourselves as well as out is an alchemy all of its own that has to do with bringing our heavenly and earthly beings together.

These two parts correspond to the two children we find in ourselves: the child of soul, or the 'golden child', and the child of history, who bears the wounds of experience. The child of history relates to our emotional nature located in the solar plexus, where the child of soul - the one we essentially are - always connects us to our hearts. Earth is an imperfect realm. It is dense. It hurts. We come here to learn, separated from the life of the spirit, but vitally, because that way also lies home.

Evoking the relationship with either parent brings out the child in us. This is part of Sol's descent into the core of himself and who he is beyond his definition as his mother's or father's son, with his own journey to accomplish. In one man's dream:

It is morning. I am standing holding a map which shows a strip of blue coastline. It is a wonderful blue, a radiant azure – and it runs along the north-western edge of *New Zealand*. Even in the dream, I am aware of it as new country, a new land. And I am going to take my parents for a walk there – *I* am going to take *them*, child as I am, rather than them taking me.

The child is always there inside us, whether we are aware of it or not. The child feels what we *actually* feel as opposed to what we should feel, or what would be convenient to feel. You may know from your own children the directness and lack of compromise they have in delight as well as in pain. The child, it is said, 'holds the soul' in us. For years before I made better contact with my own inner child, I would see him standing there in tears because of my neglect of him.

This is very different from the adult who can rationalize away what he or she is actually feeling. So, contact with this child always brings us back to ourselves, to our own feelings, and back *inside* ourselves as well – inside our body and being as opposed to somewhere 'out there' in our minds, rushing along on automatic pilot. The child can lead us, though it is sometimes important for *us* to take *him* by the hand, either to reassure him or comfort him. Part of Sol's task is to take his wounded child in hand and to feed and nurture him. We may understand this in terms of his taking responsibility for his emotions. When the wounded child is given healing, he can be golden again – he can tell us what he needs and he can lead us along the ways of renewal to what is most free and original in us.

## The Wild Man

Another part of Sol that he meets, or meets again, in this descending stage, beneath his sexuality, his father and his inner child, is something even older and more fundamental: the wild man.

The wild man as an archetype goes beyond biography, and yet he is individual to every man. *Iron John* tells the story of a child's closeness to a man found in the woods at the bottom of a deep pool. Robert Bly has made this famous, but this is just *one* wild man, *one* image. Each man will have his own.

The child and the wild man are perhaps closer in the psyche – as they are in this fairy tale – than they are 'in reality'. Both have vital and soulful (Sol-full?) things in common. Both tend to be in exile from the heart of a man's life and preoccupations. So it is no wonder they can talk to each other. Again, it is our clear (or 'golden') child who can be open to the wild man's message and his gift.

The wild man can be as uncompromising as the child, though in a slightly different way. Where the child shows us our true feelings, the wild man expresses what the body really feels. His depth is primordial, reaching back to a time before time, a time that is *under* time, like a cellar in a house. His language is older than words and perhaps only poetry can approximate it. In Peter Redgrove's phrase:

or was that when I was grass?[12]

Only words can bring us closer to things, or else no words at all, rather the things themselves, felt as they are rarely felt – grass, rock, water, air, the scent of it, the atmosphere in the woods, and the sense of movement at the corner of the eyes as a deer turns liquid in among the shadows of the trees...

Here is one man's account of him, in response to three simple directives:

* Imagine walking into a forest to meet him.
* See who and where he is.
* Ask him for his story.

I walk out of the sun in among tall shaded pine trees, and then down as the ground slopes and the air cools ... towards a glade and the fresh trickling sound of a spring.

And he is there: sitting with his thighs spread over a rock, clothed in skins, his hair matted and long, his feet bare on the moist fern-covered ground, his eyes poised silently as if in meditation.

He doesn't speak. He doesn't look up. He doesn't need to. He answers my presence in a language older than words or even eyes.

He is in exile, human as he once was, with a name, before the forest became his domain with him as its guardian, feeding it through his being.

I ask him for his story and suddenly he is standing in front of me. He takes my head in his hands and presses it sideways against his chest, so I can hear it for myself.

*'My story is my heart, my story is my heart...* Once there were many of us. Now I spend my days alone, in this last tract, in meditation for the Earth like the rest of my kind...'

I hear what he is saying as words in my own mind, as a bird flies down onto his shoulder.

Then he stands and takes me over to the pool under the spring, inviting me with a gesture to drink the water in my cupped hands. I take my clothes off to sit with him, feeling the moss under my skin and the air over my body, drinking the green-scented light in through my eyes, as he continues: 'I have always been here, and my story is as yours may be, to dream and dream clearly of a people who will learn how to live here fully in mind, feeling and body...'

I look down at my naked legs and reach out to touch the ground with the palms of my hands.

Then he takes me into the water and as we stand there together, he bends down, lifting his hands full of clear running water over my head. It streams down over my brow and into my eyes, down my cheeks, and onto my chest.

'By the Water of Life, I baptize you,' he says.[13]

'My story is my heart' – he means his heartbeat. He is not of the mind; he offers a spirituality that comes from inside the body rather than being imposed on it from outside. He is the word made flesh before word and flesh were separated.

He may be angry, as John the Baptist was, but he is neither savage nor violent. He cannot be, because he dwells inside the body where the body is, in its deepest sense, naturally at peace. His gift is to show us our place on Earth as sentient creatures and – potentially – as Forest Lords, not 'masters', but men who have grown to know what children sense: that our being here, our potential and its fruition are dependent on how we respond to the Earth as a natural law. If we are not with the Earth, we are divided against ourselves in continual anger and pain.

All of this brings Sol to the threshold of the man he is, who includes all of these parts. Over time we revisit these different aspects as an organic process and, as with a painting, wipe or add to them. These stages are not so much linear as a moving back and forth over the same terrain. Indeed, this is true of the Work as a whole.

## A Woman's Work

And what of Luna's work here? Everything we can say about Sol in this passage is also true for her, although in her own way. For Luna, the issue is her potency as a woman, and as a woman in herself rather than as defined by any exterior function, whether through professional work or domestic motherhood. Coagulation is about who *she* is and what she needs to develop. It emphasizes *her* aloneness, as it does his, and gives her the freedom to be exactly where she is. Like Sol, Luna needs to find her own clarity, directness and will while at the same time her element is different from his, just as her internal fluids are.

To a certain extent, Luna's work is a re-examination of the masculine, just as Sol's is of the feminine. This stage involves a development of their contrasexual selves, which is vital for the 'wedding' - for the real union that is potential between them. So Sol becomes more masculine by embracing his feminine side, Luna becomes more feminine by embracing her masculine side. This can create a curious discomfort, because in many ways at this stage *he is more like a woman and she is more like a man.*

Luna's own parental influences are significant in accepting her masculine aspect rather than projecting it onto Sol (or any other man), and of course her relationship with her father is significant here in terms of how much he has recognized her, just as her relationship with her mother will reflect her relationship with her own body. Here again, her childhood experience will be relevant, as will that of her inner child.

But most of all, in terms of her power, what matters here is her wildness, her old 'wild woman', who also invites her to open to a larger dimension of her own gender, to open to the Goddess and, closer to home perhaps, it also invites her to own her *witch.* It doesn't mean she has to literally become a witch, though that is a path for some people. The important thing is what this energy means to her, how accessible it is and what it may need.

Each woman has to assess this for herself, but it is clearly about contact with the feminine, a deeper feminine than she may have known.

This may also involve her exploring *her* repressed lesbian side, her love of the feminine, and examining her own relationship to her body as a woman. As with Sol, Luna may initially project this outwards before recognizing it in herself, or it may come into her dreams.

In *coagulatio* alchemy shows Luna as holding a red lion on a leash. This image describes her coming into her power and being able to 'hold' it. As Sol's work with the snake (that represents his sexuality) begins, so does Luna's with the red lion.

Luna needs to be true to herself and she needs to feel she can be separate rather than dependent or enmeshed. Sol, if he is wise, will let her be. If he doesn't, she will have to claim her need more forcefully, which may also be part of her initiation. Some of what she may need to contact here is her rebellious adolescent, which has to do with being individual and separating out, as we know. A woman who hasn't lived her adolescence will tend to find herself doing so here. The pain of her actual adolescence may also resurface, alongside a mercurial youthfulness – she can look half her age!

She can't be true to another unless she can be true to herself. That means *not* being pliable and manipulated. She may need to say No to release an inner strength that means she can say more of a Yes. This is part of her *illuminatio*.

Also, she needs to nurture herself in all senses, including literally in what she eats: real food as opposed to junk food. This is her *nutrimentum*. Self-love here for her is hands-on, it is practical. This can include self-nourishment through seeing and being with friends, widening the web. Our lack of self-love can leave us too isolated. Feeding ourselves also means being a friend to ourselves. This is where loving ourselves may need to begin. What Luna finds here is that she can't love Sol in any real way –

beyond being a romantic or temporary image – unless she loves herself. She can't love or find ground with him.

*And then there can be a softening between them as they sit up in the open field together, feeling the warmth of the air, the birdsong and the ground.*

*Then the warming touch between them allows her to feel safe, not pressured or invaded, and for him to feel touched without it having to be sexual, even as he lies over her, clothed as they are, as she savours the weight of him and the firm grassy ground under her...*

## Coagulatio

**Context:** Grounding/coming into form and foundation, differentiating as man and woman, marrying ourselves within

**Key question (for chapter 5 also):** What is the earth inviting you to here? What does it mean to come into a greater reality?

You may also hold this question in terms of your personal history and consider how much you have integrated or made peace with your past -and how much you are still rejecting it ?

Taking the two main stages, Venus and Mars, here in sequence:

## Venus

*Men:* What does potency mean to you as an inner reality – as opposed to having power 'over' something or someone else? If you take this into meditation, see if you can allow an image for potency to arise, and then come out and draw your image.

Reflect then on what it is saying/showing to you; and what it needs from you. (You can 'ask' your image, and see what comes intuitively as a response.)

*Women:* What does being in touch with your own power mean for you – and how do you relate it to your experience of being a woman? You may also take this into a space of meditation and visualization, allowing an image of potency to come.

Then reflect as above.

*Men:* What does it mean for you to nurture yourself without depending on a woman (or mother figure)? How do you or might you do this?

*Women:* What does it mean for you to nurture yourself without depending on a man (or father figure)?

**for both of you, then:**

What does it mean for you to see your relationship in more earthly terms?

And what does it mean to see each other as companions on a journey?

What does the Beloved mean to you as a higher source of love beyond your partner?

Reflect on your experience here of greater love, also in terms of other people you know.

Reflect on your sexual history and how you have been as a sexual being within it (discuss with partner). Hot, cool, pleasing, performing, nervous, terrified? What might healing mean here?

*Men:* Reflect on your relationship with your father . What did you receive from him? What do you need from him – and what does he need from you?

*Women:* Reflect on your relationship with your mother. What did you receive (or not receive) from her? What does she represent for you about your own experience of being feminine?

**Try this:** sort and order family photographs as an expression of your life as a way of reflecting on where you came from, what is behind you, and what your developmental challenges are in this sense.

**Try this:** actively keeping a journal or 'log book' at this stage, which may also contain illustrations if you are visually orientated towards drawing, painting or photography. Your log may also be in the form of a sequence of poems, where the unconscious as well as your feelings may speak more directly.

**Try this:** consider your diet and what you are taking into your body in terms of health and energy, including nicotine or alchohol. Evaluate your diet in terms of acidity, and the effect this may be having on your emotional state. Consider what supplements you may also need as well as getting allergies (especially wheat and dairy tolerance) tested.

You might try going on a wheat and dairy free diet for a month, making sure you drink plenty of water, while also taking vitamin and anti-parasitic supplements.

Chapter Four

# Erotic Soul Relationships

*coagulatio*

Venus

Our problem in relationships is how to have an on-going,
intimate life with another person at the same time as we invite
this completely unpredictable depth to have a significant place
in our lives...
– Thomas Moore

Here at this stage in coagulation we need to explore more of what
we mean by freedom. The core issue, the single reason why
relationships have repeatedly broken down, links to what is most
fearful and perhaps least loving in us, but what defines a traditional relationship. The issue is *exclusivity*.

This means you can't be with her if you are with me. At least
that is our assumption. In fact it is our hope and indeed expectation every time we enter a relationship. This time it will work.
This time I will be favoured. This time I (and it) will be the one.
It is not wrong to wish for this. But is it love?

By exclusivity, what we also mean is *exclusive body rights*. Your
body is reserved for me. If you  share with someone else what
you share with me, I will assume you do not love me and respond
accordingly.

We are confronted here with a paradox, one that is in the word
'exclusive' itself. It excludes in order to define. But then what it
defines means that feelings which cannot in reality be excluded
*are* excluded. The emphasis, rather than being on privacy and
keeping in, becomes one of keeping out. This is our relationship:

*keep out.*

We want safety. We want assurance. We want certainty and commitment, of course. And we also want challenge, risk, adventure – we want freedom. And if we love the one we're with, we want them to have those things as well. But who are we to say what that might mean for the other person? It can be a startling thing to realize that freedom is not ours to give.

And love, if it is love, if it is centred in the heart, means what it says: *'I can love you , but I can never possess you. You do not belong to me, you belong to yourself'* – or we might say, *''You belong to Love.'* And it recognizes that without the freedom of the other there can be no love – a lesson it seems we are all having to learn at this time (the present author being no exception).

So, insecurity is a part of life. Anything can happen at any time. Must this include betrayal? It may. The uncertainty principle is part of life, because if we knew how everything was going to be we could not create and we would not feel. This is the gap, the void which creativity demands, that is also the space that brought the loved one to us in the first place – and could also take them away.

As James Hillman explains:

We can be truly betrayed only where we truly trust – by brothers, lovers, wives, husbands, not by enemies, not by strangers. The greater the love and loyalty, the involvement and commitment, the greater the betrayal.[1]

And as he adds, on a deeper note:

And betrayal, as a continual possibility to be lived with, belongs to trust just as doubt belongs to a living faith.[2]

The only way we can avoid being devastated here is to accept, without resignation, that what our loved one needs to do might not be what we want them to do. We may not know, at least for a time, what they might choose to do. We would like to have the reassurance of guidelines. But love seems to require uncertainty and unknowing.

What are our usual responses when confronted with this? If we look closely, or even from several feet away, we will see they are often based not on love at all but on territorial posturing, fear and conditionality – or 'emotional terrorism':

- 'I don't like it – it makes me feel insecure.'
- 'If you do that I will divorce/leave you.'
- 'I will only love you *if...*' (not simply because you exist)
- 'I can only open to you *if...*' (a more subtle version of the same)
- 'When I think of her, I want to kill her!' (Naturally!)

In a word, we regress. And yet these are the responses we still expect. They are even vaunted as signs of true love ('I wouldn't love you if I didn't feel this strongly – this proves it, doesn't it?')

I am not saying we have no right to feel these things. What I am saying is that it is time to recognize what these responses are and to ask ourselves whether we want to go on responding and acting in these self-limiting ways.

These are the responses of the primitive brain. Fight or flight. Or, in a slightly more advanced sense, *barter.* Cajole, plead, manipulate. And if it's not working, *bully.* Unconditional love simply doesn't make sense to the old brain. There are also the more subtle aspects of shaming here, taking the moral high ground and seeding guilt in our partner's mind. And we have to get beyond this to expand into a bigger picture, a greater loving. We have to keep coming through into the heart.

Where does this begin? It may start with the simple recognition that however exclusive we may be, there are *never* just two of us in a relationship, there is always a third 'body' which connects everything we have experienced in our lives and everyone who has been a part of that. So there are not just two, or even a few of us, there are (as subscribers to 'polyamory' also believe) *many* of us, and we all have business with each other, 'soul business' that involves different degrees of connection and feeling, different issues, difficulties, opportunities, thresholds. We can find this with so-called strangers too.

Love is broader than we tend to bargain for. And love, it seems, is a *process* rather than a cut-and-dried event. It is a story that we are not so much writing as are written in, a film, if you like, with an extremely mercurial director. Love is work, too, living unpaid work, or rather, paid only in kind. The idea that love is for pleasure and comfort alone really is a myth for the faint-hearted. The reality of our close relationships, then, becomes an expanded area where we are much more involved with each other than we may know.

## A Different Kind of Love

We know we can be attracted to more than one person and that attraction takes different forms and means different things in different contexts. Sometimes we don't know what the attraction means or what this particular relationship intends. Without words to express the subtle variations, everything, potentially or otherwise, is reduced to being a flirtation or an affair. Everything is brought down to sex because sex is the basis – the cave floor – of our animal insecurity.

This reduction blocks an expanded view of loving, keeping us all in emotional contraction, more compromised, less free, less loving. It is a vicious circle that bites back on itself, sometimes literally, as in domestic violence. We try to dam the flow and all we end up with is drought.

Sanskrit has 96 words for love: we merely have one ! We need a language for these different kinds of relationships – not just the ones we recognize as brotherly love or filial piety, but the relationships that seemingly endanger us, that make us uncomfortable.

I call these *erotic soul relationships*. They are not couple relationships, though they may sometimes become so. They are based on friendship, but a friendship that has a charged erotic quality. This quality does not have to be acted out sexually. The attraction takes place in the space between the two people. These relationships can tell us a lot about what is being left out of our lives. What has been suppressed or denied is suddenly illuminated here.

We all know these kinds of relationships, in different degrees. The Celtic tradition has a term for them: *anam cara*. As John O'Donohue says:

> *Anam cara* was originally someone to whom you confessed, revealing the hidden intimacies of your life. With the *anam cara*, you could share your innermost self, your mind and your heart. This friendship was an act of recognition and belonging. When you had an *anam cara*, your friendship cut across all convention, morality and category.[3]

It is the last sentence that is important here. Our connection may be spiritual, but it is embodied and mysterious too. So we may have immediate eye contact, the pulse of recognition and an attraction that is visual and energetic, though not literally sexual.

This is how it begins, but not at all how it necessarily remains. If we look at these relationships over time, we can see that some of them do become sexual, but equally some we think might be, or will be, turn out not to be at all. Attraction is part of what brings us together, but the purpose would, in these instances, be deflected by actual love-making. What happens instead is that the erotic element rises from the sacral into the heart as the attraction changes. Then again, sometimes the attraction remains sexual but is never acted on. It is sexual and *virginal* at the same time. This may be as a result of a conscious choice made by both people involved because of their situation, but it can also be there unconsciously, as their bodies can tell them. This can also be true for same-sex attractions between two men or women who are not actually gay or lesbian. Part of the 'soul' of the attraction is about masculinity and femininity respectively and a kind of transmission of that from man to man, or woman to woman. Support and encouragement of each other is part of what is taking place, but it isn't literally about love-making; that isn't necessary. As Joan Evans, co-founder of the London Institute of Psychosynthesis, once remarked wisely in an overall sense 'We don't have choice around love, but we do around intimacy. Love *is.*'

In this sense too we can see that - sexually or not - we can also love someone without it being right to be partners with them.

This expanded view of love may cause discomfort or relief – or something of both. As Diana Durham put it, in her poem 'Many Mansions':

If it were not so
I would have told you.

Apparently it is natural
to feel these things.

We have not understood
how large love is.[4]

As we get beyond obvious levels of emotional reaction, what we begin to understand is that both relationship and sexuality are more mercurial areas than we may have thought. 'We have not understood/how large love is' because we have insisted on looking at it in a fixed way, at a concrete level of mind which brings everything back to fear, to sex and abandonment, and so to power and punishment. As one woman expressed it poignantly in *Couples,* a recent survey:

> He won't do it again. Or anything like it. That isn't one of my worries. But I shall always wonder if it is fear of the conse-quences constraining him rather than my sexual attracti-veness.[5]

In a relationship where power takes over from love the price is that – in terms of its alchemy – *Mercurius is exiled.* Mercurius is the ambivalent factor. He/she resists definition in the name of a greater openness, a greater exploration, a greater loving. As another man put it, in a private letter

> I am sorry you felt misled. I just want to be able to explore and see how things develop in freedom without it being nailed down to expectation. Too much to ask ?

It may be useful to remember a phrase we don't have in English that is relevant here: *amitié amoreuse,* literally 'loving friendship', a friendship that can be or become sexual outside conventional partnership. Just as friendship itself is expanded by bringing in this soulful, charged aspect, so sexuality is also extended here. With Mercury, we start to understand the essence and purpose of sex.

## The Secret in Energy

Sex is energy, just as matter is. We know that in the simplest of ways. Take away the energy and the desire is gone. At a soul level, the essence of sex is a blending, an alignment of two energies to bring them into deeper sympathy, allowing a deeper level of communication. In that sense *we can  also make love to each other without literally making love.* We can touch each other's energy fields and remain there while an emotional process takes place between us, whether we are together or apart.

Our energetic fields can also be deeply affected by the constrained relatedness that is left once freedom has been denied. Our feelings remain as blockages and potentially neuroses, even obsessions. And what is true for the psyche is also true for the body. And the body can always tell us what is real if we listen to it as opposed to overriding it in a merely wilful or instinctual way. In Stanley Kellerman's phrase, 'The body never lies.'[6] True – and how often in reality do we attend to it?

Love says that we must be able to respond freely. But we may still have questions that we can't easily answer. What do we do if one of us needs more sexual contact than the other? And what if one of us is – or becomes – bisexual?

In any relationship one person's freedom affects the other and without sensitivity and honesty we can and do cause each other great pain. Merely *acting* from our freedom is not love's way. *Agreeing* to what we both want and need is a different matter, and that can be different for each couple. We need not generalize. It is not a question of legislation. We have to come into relationship with each situation as it is, which is part of what it means to be in the unknown. This doesn't mean we abandon discrimination any more than we abandon feelings, but it does mean we can be liberated from a shallow and mechanical view that turns everything into a set formula.

We need to agree our boundaries, based on what is possible for each of us, while recognizing that this will also change at different stages of our lives. In this way in our own primary couple relationship, we can *also* be soul friends – true companions to each other on our journeys rather than each other's judge or 'keeper'.

## Honesty

Remembering the stages of Venus, downwards from fermentation to nourishment and grounding, what is the basis of this? What is the ground here?

It has to be honesty, with ourselves and the other. It has to be scrupulous honesty, too, the truth as we know it. If we are dishonest with our partner, not letting her know where she stands, we deprive her of her freedom, which is one of the devious and unloving ways in which we can use our freedom against someone.

Dishonesty can inflict the deepest wounding. As one man, a well-known writer, confided, 'The real betrayal wasn't that we had had sex. It was that I didn't tell her for three months.'

Communication is, obviously, vital, since it is part of the ground. Many 'open marriages' lose their grounding and the couple drifts apart through a lack of awareness and unconscious neglect. The other aspect of grounding, one that we are constantly brought back to, is that however and wherever we are, *we are always also alone.*

We are gifts to each other, we are lent. And we, and the forms of all our relationships, are transient. To root ourselves in the reality of our aloneness is the deepest and perhaps the most courageous thing we can achieve here. There are many things we would rather do, and we all run away from this to a greater or lesser extent. But in it, we may find the greatest freedom, *the freedom to love,* and be able to find and follow the thread of love's way ... which is golden.

## Chapter Five

# New Ground

*coagulatio* – separation, differentation
Mars
'the relationship we fear and resist'

What thou lovest well remains
the rest is dross
What thou lovest well is thy true heritage
What thou lovest well shall not be reft from thee.
– Ezra Pound

Coming back to our story, where is Sol now in the process? He is more aware of his sol-itude than ever. The bigger picture has brought him, and us, back to ourselves, for we discover here that the only way we can enter this greater loving fully is *by being prepared to be alone*. Aloneness is an authentic place where we can drop pretence.

Sol's need turns inward here and this is probably his lowest point in the whole process in terms of energy. It is as if he is lying at the bottom of the flask, in a dip in the ground. Nothing is entirely clear and the sense is that this wretched process could go on forever.

Sol is waiting for his fire to return and it can only do so when he stands his ground, when he has ground to stand on. When he recognizes this he is ready to pass from Venus to Mars and so into what alchemy calls 'the solar life'...

## Mars

The first of the stages under Mars, which complement those under Venus, are:

*fixatio*
*multiplication*
*revificatio*

Immediately we are coming into something stronger and more fiery, which Mars signifies. It is through fire that mutable silver is said to aquire the constancy of gold, and that the stone, having been yellowed, is now said to 'redden'. Both of these descriptions give us a clue as to the essence of what is going on here and what the gold itself requires to come into being within us.

The Mars stage is also said to mark the end of the 'lunar life'. The emphasis now passes to the sun, which is also seen as the centre. As the Egyptian hieroglyph depicts it:

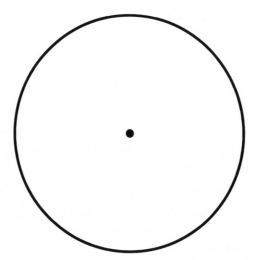

The dot is surrounded by the circle, the 'I' stands at the centre, finite manifestation is surrounded by the infinite with all its potential. That is what is seeking to come into being. In terms of our identity, it is what alchemy describes as the 'royal' part of us.

## Fixatio (doing it)

*Fixatio* is the sign of this, of the fire Sol has been waiting for. There is simple and pure action in this stage, as well as an intention that engages our will. We can think of it in the sense of committing something to paper, or sketching out a painting. *I am going to do it now.* We may, however, need to be roused or even goaded into doing it!

But then *fixatio* is also about the energy to sustain an undertaking. It is about constancy, the constancy and commitment that are necessary for gold. No more indecision: now is the time. Once the energy is mobilized, we find the strength, even under difficult conditions. It is a strength that we might have been unaware of until it is put to the test. *Fixatio* is also about standing our own ground, once a decision has been made. As the popular chant has it, 'We shall not, we shall not be moved !'

So this is where fire and earth meet. And like a fever, or like anger in the body, it is something that is substantial rather than intellectual. The heat starts to rise again under the flask and its contents, and it is here we enter what alchemists refer to in terms of temperature as 'the third degree'.

## Multiplicatio (multiplying)

*Multiplicatio* (literally, 'multiplication') follows. Here there is the sense of expansion and relief we feel when something has been achieved. We emerge into sunlight which seems to extend the sky, and with it, the sense of what is possible.

*Multiplicatio* in this sense is simply about what Richard Moss calls 'radical aliveness',[1] which manifests in such unexpected ways, like the black butterfly which landed on his forehead. We can think of it in a more everyday sense as being *in life* too:

simply shopping in town on a Saturday morning, seeing people walking, hearing the sounds of voices and street musicians and greeting the faces of friends.

*Multiplicatio* has the feeling of richness about it, of all the things we have in our life we can feel grateful for, the blessings we can forget to count. It has a spontaneity which 'multiplies', the way one thing leads to another. Because life is intrinsically generous, which we realize when we get beyond our more narrow or controlling view of it. This is what we open to here. It is the soul of new ground.

## Revificatio (coming back to life)

This brings us to *revificatio*, which is 'resurrection'. *Revificatio* is a rising then, a rising fire that we can think of as the gesture of standing, as a dancer may stand in the fullness of her feminine grace, the red stage lighting outlining the edges of her body in its leotard, poised, electric.

For Luna, *revificatio* marks the achievement of her red lion work, through which she rises into her true power. For Sol, something more vital happens in terms of their relationship: his work here is in transcending his own sexual compulsion – symbolized by the snake – so that his sexual energy rises *to become the whole of his body*. So the snake here is kundalini, the fabled gold serpent that lies coiled at the base of our spines. Its rising at this point gives meaning to the suffering of the desert journey, meaning beyond our wildest dreams.

## Coming into Form

I will consider here a number of related areas and their implications for relationship on our journey before coming to the key to unlock what we can think of as the missing dimension of marriage.

With Mars what we are negotiating is the world of form. This is a challenge, because it is a world in which we have to acknowledge imperfection and limitation, and yet without form, there would be no manifestation in reality. It is through the medium of earth, that mixes spirit and matter, that we have to achieve what we call maturity.

The question here is: *are we strong enough to make a vessel to hold the Work?* This is what alchemy calls the flask, and for our relationships it is what surrounds and holds them and allows a process to take place within them. We could say that the further we go, the stronger the vessel needs to become, otherwise the inner activity will shatter it, and this is another aspect of what we can understand by commitment, and the need for it, in an alchemical sense.

The strength is an inner strength too, that we cannot and should not project entirely onto an outer structure or place. It is a strength *we* need between us in order to bring what we have into workable form. Continuing our analogy from copper and iron, when tin is added to copper, it makes a stronger metal, bronze. There is a threshold of commitment here, even if it is not 'full' (or complete) as yet.

In terms of relationship, this is both an individual and together task. We really need to see all these Mars stages 'bifocally', just as we do relationship itself, in terms of our relationship with ourselves and our relationship with our partner. We must have both.

Relationships commonly break down at this stage, when the gloss of romance has gone, revealing instead a scratched bare surface. This is where we can be tempted to give up and move back into a *coniunctio* , a new beginning with someone else, even having survived *nigredo*, which is the obvious place to separate. *Solutio* has its own temptation, which is to stay in dream and not enter reality. *Coagulatio* has its special difficulty, which is finding a form that is specifically appropriate, helping the relationship to grow rather than stagnate. We may first have to work through forms from the past, that are not helpful to what we need now.

We need to realize what can go wrong. It can, for instance, be like buying a house. To start with you need to appreciate it, to admire its shape and texture, its atmosphere. You need to be able to imagine what it could be like living there. But then a different phase begins at the point where you must decide whether to go any further. Then you find yourself looking over it in a different way, as you walk round from room to room. What about that crack there in the ceiling? What about the damp? Will it be a problem if we leave it?

As all the various factors gather it can be dispiriting, even overwhelming. A certain dreaminess and disconnection may turn us away from the task in hand, and away from the world as well. We may rationalize why we *shouldn't* move forward here. This is how our fear can speak. But alchemy advises us to keep going and not be put off by 'the continual rising moisture' that takes us back to the past and its insoluble pains. We need instead to build on our own ground.

### Inner and Outer Geography

In the experience of expanding, there is an inner releasing – perhaps of what we really feel. With expansion, there is also new ground, or the old ground seen anew. This is what the experience of space, and certain landscapes and places, can give us.

I can easily bring this particular beach to mind. It is called Inch Strand, near Dingle, in the west of Ireland. It spreads for four miles in a great bow of golden white sand, with nothing but the Atlantic breaking in, wave after wave, and the mountains rising beyond, in ever-shifting layers of cloud and light. At this particular moment, having walked slowly for a long time in thought, I am turning to walk back to Lios Dana, the holistic centre where I'm staying, and as my eyes trace the contour of the headland and the silver-grey sea I know without any doubt that *love is not morality*. Love has been compromised by the structures we know, the shapes we have tried to explain, bind and tame each other in. Love is free, and nothing we have ever done or can ever do will change that. Love is itself.

Or, as Philip Carr-Gomm experienced it, this release can come as an inward awakening:

When this idea first came to me, I had to sit down. It was as if I had been looking all my life for one thing, one object, that suddenly was shattered into a thousand pieces by this one idea. But instead of being horrified, I was liberated. Somehow I'd fooled myself into thinking that there was one thing, just one person out there, who would make me happy and whole, but this idea dissolved this illusion with one blow! And out came love from every crevice and crack in my body and my life and the world out there – singing, dancing, holding onto its belly to stop itself bursting with laughter. 'Something huge in my life has just been shattered,' I found myself thinking when the laughter had subsided. 'But instead of breaking something, it's made everything whole.'[2]

With that realization comes a joyousness, comes play, comes exploration and experimentation that is the domain of Mercurius – and the opposite of getting stuck. Wherever we are stuck, it is Mercurius we need to contact to free ourselves. This may include taking time out from the relationship. Mercurius can stir, break and reinvent the mould of our thoughts. Something inside us is always reaching for the new, for *new life,* for new ground. It is that edge we are looking for, as the poet inside us knows. As Thomas Merton put it in *The Geography of Lograire*:

To have passed there
Walked without a word

To have felt
All my old grounds
Forgotten world
All along
Dream places
Words in my feet
Explain the air of all
Feel it under me

Stand
Stand in the unspoken
A cool street
An air of legs
An air of visions

*Geography.*
*I am all (here)*
*There!*[3]

It is a newness we can find in dreams, in the way that dreams 'melt' reality, opening it up to unexplored patterns and relationships. We can find it in the first minutes of waking where we are still between two worlds and our thoughts can be pictures that speak. We can find it in language in the simplest play on words, maybe a playfulness we were never allowed and do not allow ourselves. As Anna Comino-James puts in in her tiny poem 'Intimacy':

In
To
Me
See.[4]

opening up a whole meditation on the word by rephrasing it.

This newness is also in being freed from the literal – and in this sense it is like the difference between the 'letter' and the 'spirit' of the law. We can celebrate it in the glory of the Earth and all its amazing immutable processes that link one thing to another in an artistry we often neither know of nor see, where, as we say, truth is stranger than fiction.

All reality is subjective. What we claim as fact is also an interpretation. Someone else will have interpreted it differently. And we can both be right. This is true in relationship wherever we find ourselves on two sides holding different points of view. We can oppose each other or we can listen – and learn to let each other in. It sounds so simple and can be so difficult. But it is so much easier when we realize *we alone, individually, cannot have the whole truth.*

Our very identity is based on exclusion, in the sense of what we leave out. We are *this* because we are not *that*. We are all (like this book) an edited version of reality. In this sense new ground can be unsettling and unnerving, as any open system is, because it brings us to a reconceiving of ourselves and our frames of reference.

But the reality of our body and being is one of constant movement anyway, with our bones, in our blood, our cells being replicated. Our personality, too, is a changing flux. And beyond this? We are also multi-dimensional beings all the way from our dream self to our conscious self, our primitive self to our psychic self, our earthly self to our star self. We are so much more than we know. At a psychological level, *we are also what we have suppressed.* This also belongs to our lives and may hold a key to what we experience at this stage of the process.

What have we *not* identified with in our lives? Do we need to open ourselves to something we have suppressed or rejected? In relationship we may have to face this, consciously or not, through a kind of creative opposition. One of us may be looking at something that the other needs to, and isn't, or hasn't.

As one man writes:

> I was so preoccupied with her thinking about herself as a
> lesbian I forgot to think about my own repressed
> homosexuality that had caused me (although in a different
> way) just as much anxiety. As I started to dream about being
> with men – something which would have been abhorrent in
> reality – I started to come to something in myself, to a greater
> presence and warmth with my own body ... more a sense of
> being in my body as a man, rather than always reaching
> towards her as the body I wanted to be with.[5]

The issue could be money, too. You, for instance, may need to
explore letting go of a well-paid job in order to develop other
gifts, while I need to take on earning money as part of valuing
and experiencing myself in a more expanded as well as practical
way. Here again we are both extending our lives and both
challenges will make us feel uneasy, because the ground is not
familiar. So we are both learning new dance steps to music we
don't so easily recognize.

Fear, of course, will interrupt the flow. This is where the
concrete mind is the opposing energy. Above all, the concrete
mind (which takes everything literally) can be haunted by a lack
of trust and burdened by what it believes can only be repeated
from the past. This is a kind of reverse *coagulatio* where again
Mercurius will be exiled and we can be retrenched in our
positions as separate and opposed people.

## Lightening Up

To avoid this, we may simply *lighten up*. There is a lightness of
being that comes with play and which is essential here.
Otherwise it can all get too heavy, too psychological. We can
over-analyse, at a huge cost. We can talk a dream or a good idea

away. This is the shadow side of our self-conscious and narcissistic age. Like too much chocolate it becomes its own addiction – without the sweetness.

In the case of a relationship between a therapist and consultant, he played the therapist and she was alternately client and then therapist in return. It was a disaster. They ripped each other apart. This brings up the issue of whether psychological interpretation is always helpful. I am reminded of something the Irish meditation teacher Bob Moore said that has always stayed with me: 'You can't solve a problem at the level of the problem.' You need to go to another level, where its effect can provide a more permanent release.

This is where detachment begins to enter. Because it's here that we need the means to stand back and not only see peripherally (round the issue, with a broader view) but also simply *let go* and lighten up. Mercurius again! The Lightener here. So let us find something simple that can carry us through the problem area. What we can do that we can simply agree on? It may be walking together, or dancing, or seeing a film, or a combination of any of these – anything that doesn't pressurize the relationship (like sex, or nit-picking...)

This is part of the refining fire of this stage, because it is something we also have to choose and allow into being, so heaviness doesn't get the upper hand. And it takes a willingness to let go, as well as a selflessness – knowing when to shut up and stop going on and on like a needle in a groove. Thank God for humour! Five seconds of laughter can do more to loosen the solar plexus than an hour of cognitive agony...

*And the light pours back into your eyes and your mouth.*

## Letting Go

There is another dimension of lightness that also challenges us and takes us further: letting go. What does letting go mean in relationship? It is holding the other lightly and always being prepared to release him or her, never forgetting that we are also separate beings. Rainer Maria Rilke puts it well:

> We need in love to practise only this: letting each other go. For holding on comes easily: we do not need to learn it.[6]

This doesn't only apply to the one we love: it is true for anyone we are in relationship with. It is especially necessary when we are confronted with something we don't understand and can't explain – when someone does something unexpected, chooses not to contact us, not to return our calls. We wonder why. We may feel aggrieved and hurt. We may want to say so and that may be appropriate. It is not an excuse for lousy behaviour, but what we are confronted with is still their mystery and their separateness, which we can neither change nor control.

This is where all the stories of unrequited love belong, in the mystery of a love that cannot or can no longer be returned. And what we see is there is a *wordlessness* here, just as there is when a relationship is dying. There is a wordlessness like a wall of light we can't penetrate.

So it can be all the more jolting to be reminded of this with someone we are with – and yet there is something there that feels the same, even though the situation may be quite different.

Here again we realize we can only love each other unconditionally, for conditional love is always putting pressure on the other – to be available, to be accountable, to be predictable – so that we feel safe. We may have to be forcefully reminded of someone's difference and their mystery, shocked into realizing what letting go means.

Letting go is an initiation, then, as well as a lightening. What it also enables the other to do is *to return to us freely*. This is what 'letting the other be' also means – renouncing all our secret mechanisms of control. These are what burn away here, in the light that goes beyond the flame, the growing light that is also the gold.

While this is not the end of love's way, it can allow us to expand our horizons and extend our own love into friendship.

## Friends

This opens us to friendship in a new way, in terms of what it means to let our partner be our friend and treat them as a friend. 'Friendship,' as we wisely say, 'is the bottom line.' Without it, where do we turn when things are really difficult? We can fall out of relationship, with tremendous bitterness, and the other can become like a stranger overnight. Separation can be like a sword or knife, as opposed to a process we both collaborate in with gentleness and grace.

It can be incredible to see how people who apparently know and have loved each other well have never really become friends. It is as if that quality has been taken for granted – and it should never be. Friendship needs cultivating like a garden, especially friendship between lovers. And the only road to friendship is acceptance – which also means acceptance of separateness and all that goes with it.

Our friends give us a feeling of where we are in the world and in the wider sphere the world represents. And they are vital points of reference for us in our development, as we are in theirs. It is important that we *see* our friends, that we expand the circle of our friendships and do not restrict each other as partners in this.

Friendship is an acknowledgement that *we* are on a journey – a broader 'we' that we two are a part of. If, as ecologist David Abram suggests, one of the problems with relationship now is that it puts a burdensome expectation on the other that ultimately only Creation itself can satisfy, then we can see how important friendship is. We are courting an early death without it, as too many passionate relationships have discovered.

We are held by the wider web – and that is part of the greater loving, as well as our way further into it.

## A Man's Work

Coming back to Sol for a moment again, what we see in all of this is a man being brought to the root of his own power: in his emotions, his sexuality, his body, in how he is and what he does, in what he allows and where (for himself) he draws the line. He has to be separate in order to feel this, to feel his own masculine being rather than his attraction to Luna, even as his work also takes place alongside her and in interaction with her. At the end of the desert journey, he emerges as *something more than he has been,* having passed through earth and fire.

Alchemy describes this as a physical awakening in soul that is also the spirit coming into and through the body. Earth rises to heaven, heaven descends towards Earth. Sol descends into earth and water, and then rises in fire and air.

## The Meaning of Opposition

The fire of Mars is a refining fire, as we have seen, very different from the black fire of Saturn and the *nigredo.* There are connections, but also differences: where Saturn breaks down or deconstructs, Mars re-creates and builds up. But what Mars builds up is an *inner* quality, an inner form, even if it also involves an outer structure like a work schedule or a building. This brings us back to boundaries as an expression of the body of a relationship and to 'opposition' as the energy with which they are created.

We know Mars as the god of war. Here the fighting is internal. It may be between us as well, but it is us essentially a *struggle within ourselves.* As Sri Aurobindo once put it:

This hidden foe lodged in the human breast
Man must overcome, or miss his higher fate.
This is the inner war without escape.[7]

This 'hidden foe' is sent to try us by being our opposite. We can think of it as the shadow and also the dross – the opposite of the gold – which we are here to transform. But without it, alchemy says, there would be nothing *to* transform. It is through it that we can find the way. We need our opposite in order to become truly ourselves. It is what we come up against, both in ourselves and, in relationship, through another. If we can recognize this, then the partnership struggle can become very fertile ground.

*The issue is boundaries. They come back from a walk by the river. It has flooded its banks and the towpath has turned to water they have had to wade through up above their ankles. The surrealism of it as well as the memory of their laughter stays with him.*

*The plan was for him to leave. On impulse he suggests staying to eat, but she has a friend coming for supper whom she wants to see alone.*

*He feels she is being too uptight and unspontaneous. She feels he is being insensitive and invasive. He feels she is being closed. She feels he is not hearing her 'No.'*

A typical everyday situation. How could we see it differently?

They are holding the opposite truth for each other.

He is holding fluidity and spontaneity that lives in the moment. She is holding structure and time that honours intentions. He needs to come back into himself. She needs to open to herself.

And if one of them can move, then the other can also. And then the other aspect can be revealed. Then – having separately come back to themselves – they can be side by side.

Meanwhile the river remains the river, with the flooding path ebbing behind them, and we cannot say what it means without taking both their sides.

This is the practical work of daily reality; it is the forge of a relationship's emerging form. It is where we need to be separate for a shared foundation to come into place. We need to be honest, too, about what we are feeling – half-truth dampens the fire.

## Boundaries

Boundaries don't come in ready-made sizes. We each have to find what feels right for ourselves. We can be over-boundaried at one extreme, or boundless on the other, or somewhere between these two, as on a slide-rule, where who we are will change according to what's happening. But unless we know our needs, and the needs of a relationship are understood and established, we will often find our boundaries by default – negatively, by finding them invaded or by finding ourselves isolated.

Boundaries are often in the shadow of a relationship, perhaps closer to soul than spirit in this sense, to what is deeper in the body and less accessible to view. This is where communication is so important, so we can take on what the other is holding for us, while recognizing that is also what they are struggling with themselves. Then we can also come to a deeper understanding of what is going on in terms of our *internal* opposition.

The partner who is 'over-boundaried' is likely to be so because there has been invasion, or fear associated with boundless experience. So they need structure. Equally, the partner with looser boundaries may be emerging from a period where the feeling has been one of deprivation and being 'held in'. Each is reacting to an opposite.

This is why we have to make allowances, we have to let each other over-compensate to some extent. We're not going to get anywhere otherwise, other than back into perfectionist judgement which freezes everything into white. As Robert Bly put it in 'After Listening to the Köln Concert', his poem which has Keith Jarrett's mercurial improvised piano as its background:

When men and women come together
how much they have to abandon![8]

Yet it is not enough to simply compromise and settle for less than is needed.

Through all of this we need to achieve a practical and detailed knowledge of each other in terms of how we respond, while recognizing that it is only equality and a constant attending to the other which works. In this sense, the flask of a relationship has many compartments, just as a mansion has many rooms. In opening up those rooms we may create a palace, a house for the richness of all that can be between us.

In terms of opposition, this means *realizing that the other is also ourselves.* Then what is between us can move, while we retain the tension that makes each other who we are. We may call it a dance, because it is both a holding and a letting go, a withdrawing and a coming forward from moment to moment, but now it is not just a dance of music and soft lighting, it is a dance in the light – a Sun Dance for lovers – with an intuition which is informed, rather than hopeful and blind.

### Being Royal

Alchemy likens this Mars stage to being penetrated by sulphur – Sol's element, that is the reddening stone and the approaching sun that is the gold. We stand in our own fire, seeing that what is trying to emerge, or re-emerge, is our 'inner king and queen'. As Bly says, simply:

The inner king is the one in us who knows what we want to

do for the rest of our lives, or the rest of the month, or the rest of the day. He can make clear what we want without being contaminated in his choice by the opinions of those around us. The inner king is connected with our fire of purpose and passion.[9]

The king's decisiveness is the right we all have to feel what we feel and choose as we do. It is what moves our lives to the core. It is fire in the heart, like the fire at the centre of the Earth. The inner king or queen can be awakened by whatever 'fires us up', whether it is personal, spiritual or political. Yet we cannot take this part of ourselves for granted. It needs sustaining. And this is where we need our warrior energy – our Mars energy.

This royal part of us is simultaneously beyond and within us. It is fed by spirit and it lives in our hearts – and guts. This is what alchemy means by our true identity, which is something very different from vanity of any kind. It is our own inner richness and standing, and we need to own it to find the fullness of who we are. It is the opposite of our alienated lack of belonging. And it lies at the heart of our relationships in their awakened state and potential. It is where power and love finally combine. We need to know this now more than ever, at every level of our lives. It is the key to our future evolution.

### On the Threshold

At this point we stand on the threshold of choice, of really choosing to be with our lover, of making an active commitment and standing by it. Separation may emerge here as a positive choice, so our relationship can shift to another level. The choice has to be made in freedom, with space and without pressure. And of course the other must be given that privilege too.

No pressure, but might there be a sense of urgency? This is an opportunity, an opening that will not last forever. That is the incentive. We will otherwise stay on the fence. This may be reflected by an outer situation in a variety of manifest ways. Take buying a house for instance. He may be buying it for her as well as for himself. He may want it for both of them so they can take this further step. That is fine – but he still has to choose it for himself, *with or without her.*

'If you do this, then I will' doesn't work here. We may try it. But ultimately, the choice has to be unconditional. It cannot be a choice of contingency or dependence. We have to make the choice for ourselves. Again, the strength we need for this is in the fire.

*Suddenly he remembers their first ever conversation of any length. She is asking him what he wants, or hopes for. He talks about a marriage and maybe children. Then he asks her.*

*'I want to be met,' she says simply.*

In moments like these, where real appreciation and understanding follow, we may begin to feel what it is like to be crowned – for all our upper senses to be open, around our head, while linking us to all that is below.

## Truth and Potency

Being our 'royal' selves is also connected to being true. To being truthful. This is all the more poignant in our culture of lies, where not only can we tell half-truths (or white lies) but are expected to do so in the name of 'getting on'. However, the trouble with lying is that we can't compartmentalize it. Lying spreads into everything we do. It becomes habitual, a way of life, a way of presenting ourselves as we want to be seen, so we need not face the pain of who we really are. Because it is humbling to see or be seen in our backsliding. Truth is humbling – as mortifying as it is exalting. And what if our lies are hiding a truth that the other needs to know? What if we are concealing our truth from them? This in turn connects to the issue of potency, which for both our lovers is a final refinement of the power struggle.

Just as we have to choose for ourselves here, so we also need to find our power for ourselves – and without depending on, making demands of, or blaming the other. Again, we have to face our own opposition, which will be fear. It is said that the opposite of love is fear. But the opposite of power is *also* fear. If we look at owning our own power, that fear is what we will always find, whatever the circumstances.

*His fear of being controlled. Her fear of being overwhelmed. Her fear of either being powerless or too powerful. His fear of being overwhelmed – by her, by her critical self.*

Fear is also what rises in the fire – like fragments of blackened paper turning to heat sparks and ash.

To deal with this, Sol and Luna need to turn to themselves, to turn away from the other's process and fully into their own – and to look squarely at what separates them from their king and queen within.

Sol may find, as many contemporary men have done, that this is about saying 'No' to the feminine, not automatically being nice, available, and understanding. Otherwise his fire is dampened, and Luna doesn't meet the resistance she also needs. This is what makes the king in so may men weak, because their simple 'No' is (understandably) confused with rejection. But rather, if we explain, most women will say they don't feel rejected at all, but that we are being clear with them.

In this stage both Sol and Luna may be confronted with their own power in a completely distinct way. They may have to face the opposite of their love through being opened to their *hate*. We often imagine the one we hate to be more powerful or potent than ourselves. Their behaviour to us may even endorse this. So, an image is built up, a projection that can also tell us what we may be missing and what our resentment is about. The more virulent our hatred, the less potency it indicates in ourselves.

Roselle Angwin put the problem in a nutshell to me: 'How to stay open-hearted *and* in your own power – that's the thing, isn't it?' It certainly is. Without it, we don't have the power to love.

Once again, what is required is to let each other be, which is a final relinquishing of power over each other. Letting you be is also in recognizing that *you must feel what you feel* in order to be yourself – otherwise your desire is based on appeasement or duty, a stereotype of a man or a woman, and not the real person. If we want true desire, if we want *eros* between us, we must let each other be.

\* \* \* \* \*

There is a *coniunctio* here for our couple, just as there was in the last stage, when they 'meet again'. One famous illustration shows them standing in their potency, with the figure of an alchemist between them, on earth, grounded in the instinctual realm, and at the same time tied by a chain from the wrist to the spheres of heaven above them.

We can read it like a Tarot card: here are two individualized beings, distinctly as well as nakedly masculine and femine, distinctly sensual too, in touch with the unconscious and what goes beyond, which 'holds' them.

And as Diana Durham's 'Many Mansions' continues, three-and-a-half centuries later:

*seeing you again*
*I realize how strong I must have grown*

The transition from love
to love

I'll do anything for you
except be untrue

*and the pawn became a queen*[10]

We can see our couple in a long-term relationship here, perhaps living together as well. They may even be married – the Work can be as much the story of a marriage as a relationship on its way to being so – but the guiding thread that allows their relationship to be all it can be is a very different kind of wedding: the one we make alone.

## Marrying Ourselves

Marrying ourselves is what we do in the desert. It's the desert because we'd rather not go there. It's something we'd rather not do at all. We know instinctively that it's difficult, and it is. Nothing in our culture encourages us to be deeply ourselves, as popular romantic films, however charming, like *Notting Hill* continue to show. At best, solitude or the company of a flatmate is something we put up with until 'the real thing' happens.

And yet in the real world outside cinemas increasing numbers of people are living alone. This may be by choice and it may be by default. When I lectured on alchemy at St. James's, Piccadilly, in London, a woman in the audience asked me: 'Can someone on their own do the process or do we have to be with someone?' Her question stayed in my mind.

The answer is in the inner marriage. It seems this is something we are being asked to achieve at this time. It is something that can be forced on us, through illness or accident as well as break up. I would say it is something we are *also* being asked to do in relationship, in parallel, and that in future relationships cannot and will not function without it.

We have seen so far that the inner marriage means being in

relationship with ourselves as well as our partner, but how do we do it? The image in Jungian psychology is archetypal and involves bringing anima and animus – or our female and male parts – together. But I have an argument with this. The inner marriage is certainly about our masculine and feminine, but it doesn't happen simply by visualizing a man and a woman, although a visual image may help. I once saw a man and a woman going into a long barrow to make love, and that did help. But it wasn't the thing itself, any more than touching your erect or moist genitals means you love yourself. Object images – for instance a sword and a chalice – can be more helpful because they don't split us the way a masculine and feminine image can do, making us feel that the other is always beyond reach. But essentially, we need to see this process in terms of energy rather than image. Above all, we *need* to *feel* it. Or all we have in reality is an aching loneliness.

There are many emotional factors involved in what prevents us from marrying ourselves. Objections include:

- 'I have to be with someone else. I only have half a life otherwise.'
- 'I am not good enough as I am. With him/her I feel different.'
- 'Being alone is a failure. Even a difficult relationship is better than this.'
- 'Loving myself has no meaning if I can't be with someone else.'

Here it seems that although we are alone, we are still in a relationship – *but the other is not there*. The other is a ghost. This is the same attitude that makes us dependent when we are in relationship. We are always focusing on the other, always desiring the other (sexually, too). We have to let go of this, just as we do of each other, and settle into the warmth of ourselves.

Following on from this is containment, being in the flask itself. Now it is our body. How do you feel about your body? You may say, 'Terrible.' But it is what you are sitting or lying in. It is where you are.

A third step. You are not just your body. You inhabit it with feelings, as well as thoughts. You inhabit your body *sensually*.

Fourth: your body is the flask, its feelings are the world. You are not separate. Your body is part of nature and will die. Your feelings are part of the heartbeat of everything that is alive. Your mind is part of centuries of thinking. Your higher mind takes you beyond the visible realm, just as your dreams take you below waking.

*Where are you?* What does it mean to think *your* thoughts, to feel *your* feelings, to experience *your* body? Is it void? Is it empty? No – there is a fullness that is you, a presence that doesn't go away. Your awareness is with you. You are with yourself – in your body, and more than your body; in your feelings, and more than your feelings; in your mind, and more than your mind. The one you long to be with, the one you've always loved, *is with you!*

She is above you, at all the edges of your body. If you gently breathe up, you will feel her. He is below you, in the depth of your body. If you let yourself go down, right down, you will feel him.

It may take time, but you will begin to notice something.
*You are no longer alone. That ghost has become you.*

## Coagulatio

### Mars

*Men:* How good are you at making decisions and commitments? What stops you from doing this?

*Women:* What is your experience of commitment here?

*Men:* What are the things that make you feel really alive in your heart?

*Women:* What makes your heart sing - and breathe ?

*Men:* What does it mean for you to be able to restrain yourself sexually?

*Women:* How do you contain your passion? (Without suppression?)

**For both of you:**

Consider the form of your relationship. How might it need to change? How might you experiment with this?

**Try this:** Finding a comfortable position in an undisturbed space, close your eyes and allow an image for the form, as it is. Be open to what appears. Come back and make a note or sketch/drawing of what it is. Then close your eyes again and allow a second image *for what your relationship would like to be or become.*

Again come back and note/sketch/draw your image.

Compare images, and then compare your second images as well; being aware of what is being expressed through each of them.

Take it in turns, allowing a full hour if you can.

A related question here is: What might you need to make your relationship more alive? Does Mercurius have anything to say to you here, remembering that he/she represents what has been left out?

You may also consider this question through your imagination(s) in reflective silence, then discuss what you have been sensing or seeing.

And again: How much lightness is there between you? What might it mean to remember you are friends?

**Try this:** Think of things you can or could do together that relate to the last two questions in a practical way. See if you can have at least one thing on your list that you agree is a risk !

**If you are married or want to marry:**

- remember your desire to marry and what that was or is like
- reflect on your partner as someone you love but cannot control or possess
- reflect on what it means to see your partner as royal/in her or his royalty

**At the same time:** how much are you willing to be in relationship with yourself? Do you value it as much as your relationship with your partner?

**Try this:** Ask yourself what are the things you can do that strengthen your relationship with yourself?

Are you willing to make a commitment to doing them ? If so, when ?

# Chapter Six

# Wings...

*coagulatio*
Mars

Real truth and beauty is not some gloss.
It's going to surprise us.
– David Hart

In *The Text of Shelley's Death* this is what Alan Halsey has to say
about the circle of people around the poet in 1822:

> Shelley loved Jane... Williams loved Jane. Williams also loved
> Shelley, and Shelley loved Williams. There are other loves too,
> outside this inner ring. Mary loved Trelawny, and probably
> Byron, to the point of hatred. Trelawny loved Mary, and later
> Clare. Clare had loved Byron. Clare loved Shelley... These
> people are all loving and loving, loving and hating. Jane
> loved Williams and probably loved Shelley. In the later recen-
> sions everyone loves Shelley...[1]

Does this move you? Or does it simply seem like chaos? Is there
truth in it? Or is it merely bohemian illusion? Can we write it off?
Would you want to?

It seems a far cry from today's opposite ideal of 'high fidelity'
or wanting to be adored, where increasingly younger people are
said to be intolerant of anything that smacks of love involving
more than their partner. Affairs (because they are seen solely as
that) are 'tacky'. If your partner's attention wanders, you can fire
them. Relationship begins to sound more like an employment

position: be careful, or you might be out of a job.

And so the power struggle goes on, with its other agenda, *which is to make the complex simple and controllable.* But actually, despite this professed ideal, there is as much infidelity as ever, as statistics assert. As therapist Janet Reibstein reflects: '[A relationship] has to be perfect, with everything packed into it. That's what we ascribe some of the cause of the rise in affairs to. If it fails on one front, it feels like a total failing.'[2]

This is falling to earth, or, as Thomas Moore might say, 'into soul'. I would say it is falling out of control, and that it is not merely to do with coming down from an immature height. The failure is *in spirit*, in the absence of freedom. This approach fails to understand freedom as a prerequisite of desire, choice and so loving. Absence of freedom, we discover, means we have power (in a diminished sense) instead.

As another woman from the *Couples* survey says:

With Bob sexual fidelity is a big criteria of our couple. He told me, 'If you ever have another relationship, that's the end.' It makes me feel trapped because, though I do want to be in this relationship with him, I can never predict what will happen. It makes me feel controlled and constrained. I don't actually want to sleep with another man, though some days I feel that could be liberating. I just want to be released from this embargo. If I was, I am sure my commitment would be just as strong.[3]

It is impossible not to believe her.

### ...and the Shadow

And at the same time, we have to be aware of the shadow here. For all our faith or belief, we have to ask ourselves what our motivation is or may also be in any relationship we enter into.

That, in terms of love's way, is the real issue.

As James Hillman goes on to say, in his essay 'Betrayal':

> But if betrayal is given with trust, as the opposite seed buried within it, then this paranoid demand for a relationship without the possibility of betrayal cannot really be based on trust. Rather it is a convention designed to exclude risk. As such it belongs less to love than to power.[4]

He adds:

> If betrayal is perpetuated mainly for personal advantage (to get out of a tight spot, to hurt or use, to save one's skin, to gain pleasure, to still a desire or slake a need, to take care of Number One), then one can be sure that love had less the upper hand than did the brute, power.[5]

It is quite a list, and we are likely to be guilty somewhere in it. But the point he makes is clear. *What are we up to here?* As a man, what might it mean for me to hurt another man by being close to the woman he is with? What does that mean in terms of my own relationship to the brotherhood of men, and to masculinity too? How I act is critical. I could be true – and I could be very much less. Equally, what does it mean for one woman to betray another in terms of the sisterhood? What might it say about her own power over this woman and her own avoidance, perhaps, of the pain of being a deeper kind of woman?

Without asking these questions, we are first more 'in naïvety' than we are 'in love' and secondly more prone to an ideology than to reality. The reality of love demands we look at *everyone* involved in the situation. Otherwise, in Chaucer's phrase, we are 'the smyler with the knyf'.[6] We are full of charm, but unconscious. We are courtly, but not courteous. Put simply, we are 'out of heart'. We love, or so we think, *but we hurt.*

Beware the smyler with the knyf, in male or female disguise. S/he is in us.

## Triangles

We can see this in the complex situation of a triangle. One unsatisfied partner, consciously or not, draws someone else in. They may or may not be honest or open about doing so. The third person in any triangle, like Mercurius, is always a catalyst. And the problem in any triangle is that someone invariably gets left out.

There is the person, the other partner, who is excluded. And the third person can, of course, be tempted to take advantage in a situation where he or she has power. At the same time, the couple may not face what is actually going on between them, and then the third person may be used or even abused accordingly and may then become dispensable as quickly as the closing of a door.

What is the alternative to this power-based situation? It has to be openness, with real communication and truth between everyone involved – as a triad, with all three actively participating, whether communicating directly or not. Of course, the excluded partner may refuse to do this as a gesture of the only power he or she believes is available to him or her. Equally, the unsatisfied partner originally responsible may not be up to scratch, lying to one or both of the others or procrastinating endlessly. And the third person may also be colluding in this, so that the two of them behave, in effect, like a pseudo-couple which evaporates as soon as the partner 'goes home again'.

Any of the three people involved can collapse the whole situation, which is often what happens. Triangles are difficult and sometimes humiliating places to be, requiring each person to be in touch with their own feelings and their own aloneness. But that may have to be the way of it, because of the relative degree of development of everyone involved. Love, or more love, may only come later, after the fireworks have gone off and the drama has passed. It may even be years later. It may take that long for each person to see what was really going on, where the power struggle was, and what their blindness and their learning were. And then perhaps these three people can meet as friends and genuinely embrace, or even laugh – when the pain has really been acknowledged.

These structures are in themselves transformational. They are not designed to be permanent, and so, like a homoeopathic remedy, their benefit may only come later. It may be the triangle in question wouldn't even have come into being if it weren't for that particular work needing to happen. When a couple becomes too insular or stuck, the world comes in – and may need to.

The same can happen between two couples as well, although the balance is different with four rather than three people. But the issues remain, especially for the two out of the four who have instigated the connection. Now we also have *two* excluded people, and they may both be in the position of greatest reality – that is, if they can bear to talk to each other.

### Love-Chains

In all these situations, sex may or may not have been actively involved. Desire, of whatever kind, will of course have been. But what we realize eventually is that neither sex nor attraction is really the issue. *Love is the issue.* How we behave, who we are, what we are doing here and needing to learn are what it is all about. The rest is fuel to get the situation going. And with all the fear that can fly about, and all the daily drama, one thing is real – and that is the presence or absence of love .

Love is what love *does*. That is what always emerges. 'What thou lovest well remains.' The rest is perhaps partly dross – the behaviour may well be 'drossy', or simply messy – but there is something else, something much larger involved, like a restless sea. And that is what we are all doing with one another in meeting, overlapping, catalysing and interacting, like a vast chemical process involving our hearts and minds and psyches.

I remember the first time I realized this. I sat thinking simply, 'Lucy loves Jay who loves Carole who loves Jonathan – what on Earth is going on here?' And I realized we were in a *love-chain*. Then I realized, as I looked around and as time passed, that it wasn't only the four of us. These *love-chains* were going on everywhere, being woven like daisies, as common as a sparrow's song. This was what was going on, and what mattered was how we could see and understand it rather than sweeping it under the carpet as an aberration, pretending it didn't (and doesn't) really happen.

Can we see that we are all connected to each other, even in spite of ourselves, loving and hating? What might it mean for us to see this?

It is a humbling thing to recognize, as well as exalting. There is a helplessness about it that means we are in the picture whether we like it or not. The popular press loves it; it fills the gossip columns of our newspapers daily. In a recent piece in one national tabloid, the headline read: 'The Love Circuit' and under it was a family tree of well known, less known and unknown people who had all either been married, divorced, dated or had relationships with each other.[7] There were at least 50 people in the picture – a very small slice of humanity – and most of them were portrayed smiling. Surprisingly, even despite the tongue-in-cheek journalistic phrasing that you'd expect, there was an acknowledgement of what this represents.

As Thomas Merton put it, in a more serious context:

The accidents of a poor and transient existence have, nevertheless, an ineffable value. They can be transparent media in which we apprehend the presence of God in the world.[8]

The pun on 'media' seems appropriate. Because that is where we belong, in the polymorphous general dance, in what connects us all in this bigger picture. This is an image of the world we move about in every day, but here it is warmed by a penetrating reality which lives in our innermost feeling and which we carry with us wherever we go. We can think of it as not just existing here and now, wherever you may be reading this, but right across the vanishing course of our lives where all we love lives on inside us in memory and conscience, in what we have done and in what we have not done, and beyond, into the invisible realm where people we have loved have gone. Isn't that where we belong? And isn't it *here*, too?

Nor is it just a question of transferring feelings from one person to another - particular people we know reappear or 'light up' at different times in a timing that has always been mysterious.

This leads us to something fundamental that lies at the heart of the purpose of our being here: *that we are all in a process of love in all our relationships* – especially the difficult ones.

### Community

We can see this process too in how changes in family values are directly related to the existence of community, where the extended family itself becomes a 'mini community'. Community by definition – like life itself – is about being with people we are not obviously or actually related to; it is about our neighbour becoming our friend.

Community is the test of love in action. It is where love meets the world. And where there has been a divide between more conventional family and community, the extended family brings the vital issue of community where it belongs – right into the centre of our preoccupations. Community is no longer something secondary, distanced beyond the family, with its prejudice and exclusion. It is coming inside, and coming to stay.

The *extended* family – as the very word suggests – has vital implications where we go beyond the literal or concrete level of what the word means. We are *all* family in our different ways – we are all related to one another, as only radical sects (like the Quakers) have previously tended to recognize. Now, whatever our religious or spiritual persuasion may be, this realization is happening on a secular level as part of the great transition we are in.

As writer Nicci Gerrard begins, in an article called 'We're mixed up and very happy': 'This is not how I'd planned it.' She continues:

> Thirty years later and I have two children by my first marriage and two by my second. My first husband also has two more children, and occasionally my younger daughters ask me what exactly is their relationship to them: are they kind of sisters, or more like cousins?[9]

It is a wonderful expression of a blending of relationships that have been held apart, just as families have been, so that we're not sure what to call each other, but here we all are. There is a warmth here. Love is palpably present. And there is more, which is, that *love is more natural than definition,* especially when it comes to a certain kind of moralizing that 'looks down', as if from a height, rather as city planners do on parts of the country they have never actually visited. As Nicci Gerrard goes on to say:

> Family isn't just a place, a noun. It's an activity, it should be a verb. *To family:* to love unconditionally and muddle along the best you can, whatever the policy makers say.[10]

The categories of division are dissolving. Something else is coming into being, where we all belong with each other beyond these barriers of name and skin. And, perhaps, because of them as well. They are what we are transcending.

\* \* \* \* \*

One way of looking at community is through the hell of its absence and for that we don't have to look very far. We see a world where people pass each other by without pausing, where they sit in bedsits or high rises alone, too frightened to go out, and where people – as poet Norman Jope put it – 'don't live in places anymore, they live in jobs'.[11]

This is the inheritance of our post-Industrial era. Technology is rapidly changing how we can communicate, as we know from e-mail and the Internet, but without an inner change, a change of soul and heart, we are all more likely to end up in cyberspace than closer to each other.

It wasn't always like this. And we may see that cities themselves are not the problem – the ancient city of Babylon by the Euphrates had over a million occupants – it is *our attitude within them* that is.

Nearly 3,000 years ago, this is how the *Tao Te Ching* saw it:

If a nation could be small, with few enough people
Even if it had the means to produce more, they'd be useless.
Such a people would know that death is real,
And they wouldn't travel far, even if they were able to.
They would not vaunt their army or their weaponry.
They would count in their heads again, and write by hand.
Their food would be simple, but it would feed them;
Their clothes would be fine, but homely
And they would have fires in their homes...[12]

It is a statement of community, made when China was still a nation of small states, before the Empire, like an aggressive supermarket chain, took over. How can we achieve this but through a change in our relationships? What else can make the change? It cannot come through legislation. Hundreds of alternative pressure groups have discovered that. And we need to make the change. As philosopher J. G. Bennett predicted, in a talk he gave at his community in the mid-1970s:

*We are going to be compelled to love in this way or perish, because this is the only way of life that is going to be possible on this earth* [his italics]. The only hope is a total acceptance of a higher aim than our own survival, a total acceptance of our need to be related to a higher power than ourselves.[13]

This is where our relationships with each other are not only something on a private and relatively privileged scale, but part of something immeasurably greater which we need to embrace, so we can awaken. They are love stating the greatest change of all for our times, and perhaps for all time, here at the end of time...

### Soul Family

So where do we go from here? The next step is recognizing an even wider kind of family. This is *soul family*. It is the family of our choosing rather than our origin, where the links between us reach back in time to unknown areas of familiarity, real or imagined. We may or may not have known each other in a previous life, and perhaps it doesn't matter. What matters is the quality of affection here and now between us; what it can quicken, liberate, and serve.

What we do see with soul family is that it gathers naturally. People are drawn in unusual ways to each other. It is almost like a magnetic field where we can see the patterns the iron filings make, but the magnet itself is invisible. We all have stories about the ways we have met people which defy rational explanation in their elegance and timing. 'Why now?' we might ask and the answer often doesn't need words. What we need to know is that it is here in front of us.

And when communities form? They are not straightforward organisms, any more than families are. They may be held more strongly by tradition and by work than by ideologies, as numerous instances testify. But we shouldn't judge the success of a community by its absence of challenge and difficulty, any more than we should choose to leave a relationship when the going gets tough. It can be tempting to do this, especially for an outsider who may doubt a particular group of people, either through lack of understanding or because of unresolved issues around his or her own sense of belonging. Most of us have these. Many of us would secretly like to belong much more than we do. This desire is important and it is not going to leave us.

What we can say from recent history is that a community needs to be based on individuals rather than concepts and dogma. There are many reasons for this, not least that people have to *want* to be together, and if you damage that desire, you damage the community. Authoritarianism damages desire. It takes away its freedom, just as may happen in a relationship.

For this reason a community (like a relationship) needs to fundamentally recognize difference – and celebrate it too! As one friend put it to me simply: 'Some people are good at doing the vegetable garden. I am not.' Recognizing our talents and gifts is also another way of recognizing individuality.

Something else we need to recognize is that while we all need community, whether it is in the form of a peer group or a house or even a geographical area, *it cannot be ideal*. If we don't accept this, we can throw the baby out with the bathwater and end up rejecting what we may profoundly need.

As Thich Nhat Hanh wisely puts it, speaking of Plum Village, the community he initiated in France:

The principle is to organize in the way that is most enjoyable for everyone. You will never find a perfect Sangha. An imperfect Sangha is good enough. Rather than complain too much about your Sangha, do your best to transform yourself into a good element of your Sangha. Accept the Sangha and build on it.[14]

That is advice we need for a world that is coming into being.

The other way of seeing community is inwardly, not only in the sense of whom we belong to in spirit (and soul) on the inner planes, but in the space we make in our lives, the *sacred space* we operate from, the sanctuary we make our home. Home can be our powerhouse, from which we can go out into the wider community – that community that Martin Luther King dreamed of and witnessed in the Deep South as the *Beloved* Community, where the links are overtly those of love in feeling, being and action. Again, *love is what love does*. Then the Beloved can be among us.

### Where We Live

That community may be a future dream, but why not act as if it already exists? We can do this in every daily interaction, even the small things. And anyway, do we know what is important and what is not? Can we know the effects of what we do beyond a very limited radius? We see so little of what we do, even with our physical eyes. The truth is *everything matters* – life, like a great mother, makes no distinctions.

Imagine a bright or humorous thing you've done: the simplest moment of conversation or good will in your local shop. Imagine how it might move on from the cashier you shared it with to another person. Then imagine what that next person might be prompted to do with it... So it goes on.

A greater love needs to be *on* Earth and *for* the Earth – which is what the whole of this long stage represents. We are grounded then not just for ourselves, but for the Earth we need to take our love out into – our love, not just our ecological responsibility! Because again, we need to care for the planet because we *want* to, because we *desire* to, just as we can and do for our own backyard, which is where it always starts.

Then we can begin to see our community as our world, in the shape it truly is: a circle, a globe. In seeing our Earth as the crucible and flask that it is, we can recognize what all the difficulty and pain is for and why our world is on fire: to return to the oneness and flowering of its Source.

As Gary Snyder said in *Turtle Island,* his poem for America:

In the next century
or the one beyond that,
they say,
are valleys, pastures,
we can meet there in peace
if we make it.

To climb these coming crests
one word to you, to
you and your children:

*stay together*
*learn the flowers*
*go light*[15]

That is the next threshold.

# Part Three

# The Greater Work: Rubedo

**Chapter Seven**

# Living, Loving, Open-Hearted, Royal

*rubedo* – synthesis, union
'love's relationship with us'

'Heaven and Earth are full of Your Glory.'

Now we approach the final and all-important stage of loving on our journey: the *rubedo*, the red place, the sun that is the heart of our lives *in and between two worlds*.

What can we understand of this stage or state? Here is how one woman memorably experienced it while working in therapy with me:

> It was like a red sky I could see all around me, but inside – and it connected to my heart where my heart was open like a flower. And what it felt like was this: *the truth is better than I dare imagine,* far better. It was an experience of tremendous warmth, ease and reassurance. And afterwards I found myself thinking about the Comforter – you know, Christ's promise of what he would send in the form of the Holy Spirit. It certainly came from beyond me and yet it was in me at the same time.[1]

As she later told me, 'When I'm in this place there isn't any other place to be. When I'm not, I know it's there – but I don't know how to get there.'

Her last two sentences say it all, because the essence of this final stage is grace. It comes through grace. It is not something we can manufacture or demand (although we can ask and pray). It is like inspiration in that sense – it comes when it comes, with its own timing.

## Rubedo

*Rubedo* is about synthesis. It gathers all the strands of the process together, drawing in *so it can radiate out* to a vaster expanse, like the sun itself. It is a quantum leap into a unitive dimension that comes not by forcing or will alone, and it represents a final and ongoing expansion of awareness, being and connection that links us to the cosmos – both the nearer planets and further stars.

'Above and below marry', alchemy says, and they marry within us, in our blood, the living current of substance and energy that pumps and circulates through us. This 'royal' stage is very much about embodiment: the embodiment of spirit on Earth from heaven. Yet at the same time it takes us *beyond* – beyond life, beyond death, beyond love, beyond time – to where everything is alive as the essence of itself, with a permanence which is associated with the birth of the Philosopher's Stone, both in the flask and in us. This is marrying as a process as well as an event, a state of heart, mind and being we enter and re-enter and that is finally non-separation.

As Rumi says:

This time when you and I sit here, two figures
with one soul, we're a garden
with plants and birdsong moving through us
like rain.
The stars come out. We're out
of ourselves, but collected. We point
to the new moon, its discipline and slender joy...

We have these forms in time
and another in the elsewhere
that's made of this closeness.[2]

The essence of *rubedo* is a red that is as different from what has gone before as poppies rising in a field of green corn. It is a 'sparkling red vermilion',[3] as one alchemist described it, and also purple, a royal colour signifying self-worth and dignity. It is symbolized by the sun, a dot surrounded by a circle, a blazing centre of light, heat and life. Two planets are also associated with it: Jupiter, again signifying expansion, and Uranus, planet of electricity and revolution, of sudden lightning strikes and surprises that are visitations of spirit.

Alchemy tells us there is a marriage here - but there is also death. And there is birth, too. At the heart of this final stage is the paradox of bringing and holding opposites together. It is what we live with in maturity: not 'either-or', 'black or white' but 'both-and', Mercurius gesturing with both hands, palms upwards, like scales.

The birth is of the transpersonal self, which is also known and pictured as 'the child of the Work', a third body that is created from inside us *and which is the Stone we share. together.* This is the gold, too. It points to this stage as a dimension of richness after the privation of the previous stages. Paradoxically, of course, it has its own austerity, but its many images – which include for instance the queen giving away handfuls of gold coins at a table – are full of abundance as well as healing and hope. It testifies to the heart of Creation and those who are in touch with it as intrinsically generous, a generosity supposedly rare in the modern world, but perhaps its expression is often anonymous rather than self-seeking, outside the public eye, as the Divine itself tends to be...

## Mortification

But first what we have is another twist in the tale, another unexpected turning that is *mortificatio* – literally, 'mortifying'. After the struggle of *coagulatio* we expect a grand entry and a celebration, but find a lowly door or gate, and we don't so much enter it as it enters us. It's like Christ's entry into Jerusalem, not riding a horse, but a donkey. It would be a bit like the queen arriving for a state occasion alone on a Lambretta – can you imagine? Something is badly wrong.

*Mortificatio* levels all our remaining false pride. It brings us to feeling, to humanness and soul. It reminds us that death lies at the heart of life, that it is death that allows us to *feel* life. It is part of the initiation of life.

So we have death here and a contraction of energy in the flask, rather as we did in *nigredo,* but now it is for the heart. And in us? As an alchemical saying has it, 'Mortification is the key to the Rose Garden.' Mortification brings us to our core wounds, the wounds we specifically evoke for each other, the ones we tend to get caught in and repeat over and over again. Think of a fly struggling in ointment, stuck, its wings buzzing – that is the core wound reactivating itself, but also attempting to heal, to be different this time. Psychology calls this 'a maintaining cycle'; the irony of it is that it is doomed to repetition until we see more consciously what we are doing. Then we can choose to break it.

We can't, of course, change the origin of our core wounds. We can't alter the fact that they were inflicted. I can't change your mother's ambivalence about you in the womb any more than you can change my mother's absence. What can change is our *relationship* to these things. And what is mortifying here is *to have to accept the pain.* It offends our rage, our pride and our self-pity. But if we don't accept the pain we stay stuck in repetition and blame that keep our heart from opening into its fullness. It is only in accepting the pain as it is that we can allow healing to take place at a level far deeper than intellectual recognition; that is, in our feelings and in our bodies.

We are also brought to the reality of ageing and death here. Our ego doesn't want to acknowledge ageing because that also means its own death. It doesn't want to face illness, which means helplessness and impotence. It doesn't want to suffer feeling in all its depth. But the death of the ego opens us to another kind of love – compassion, 'with passion', meaning also 'to suffer with' as opposed to 'defend against'. It's typical of the *rubedo* that we should discover that passion also means suffering – and not just personal pain or inconvenience. That is its reality.

The slightest thing can allow such feeling to come into being or to return to awareness. Think of someone you love bleeding – *it may only be a nick, but as you sit suddenly his trouserleg is red and underneath the cloth, the torn flap of flesh he is trying to staunch, it will not congeal ... and all you have in the world is a pathetic small plaster to put over it.* That was my father again, and in that moment, with the inside of his leg both the replica and origin of my own, his fragility and preciousness flared in front of me in my recognition of his mortality. I loved him then as I do now, more acutely than I could have imagined; and that night he did what he'd never done – he spoke a poem to me in my dream:

> I witness this in earth
> My scourge
> Spoken of in flowers.
>
> I'd never realized
> How deeply she could turn me
> Into her peace.

## Sol and Luna

In our story, Sol and Luna are mortified here; they are 'eaten by the starry lion'. This is another death in some ways reminiscent of *nigredo* (where the green lion is shown devouring the 'sun' of the intellectual mind), but different. The implication here is that through this narrow gate the lovers become open to a wider sphere. Their relationship cannot be a marriage otherwise. They may be close but not close enough: we can stay on the edge of this realm with a certain egoic separateness still intact. Here we are invited further and it's as if something *between us* comes apart, and as if all the unresolved threads and issues are out of our reach. We have no idea how all this can be resolved. It's like falling short of the summit. There's nothing we can do but hand it all over to a higher level. And the conundrum remains: how can we get married (or stay married) *when there's nothing left to marry with?*

Alchemy pictures this as a withdrawal of sexual energy – again in preparation, but you'd be forgiven for thinking it feels more like total defeat.

One other area recurs here that also links us to the wider community of our being. In *mortificatio* we may also have difficulty with our *other* relationships in the present, or from the past as well, where there has been hurt. Issues surface or resurface, again bringing a rawness of feeling as well as an opportunity for healing. Once more we have to dare to let down our defences. But that daring that can be illuminating – light can literally come into our minds and eyes, where we might have anticipated humiliation. And, of course, it brings us closer together again.

True forgiveness and release can't take place unless we admit we have done wrong, saying the one thing that breaks our defence: *'I'm truly sorry.'* And as we do, the hurt we confess to can be freed like an embedded splinter and there can be *at-onement*.

## Transition

'Heaven comes to us' – that is what we begin to sense here. It is not just that we go, or have to go, towards it. Something else is working here, something that may be beyond our reckoning. But we can see it, perhaps even if we don't readily believe it. We can glimpse it written on the fabric of the living air around us, flashing its being to us in sign after sign...

*You stand motionless at the edge of the field looking over to the edge of the wood where a roe deer stands motionless looking at you. Neither of you moves.*

*Out of the window, in the paddock over the roof of the house below, a heron stands in the golden evening light, a slight breeze ruffling its stationary wing feathers. It goes on standing there.*

*We rest simply on the bed clothed as we are, side by side...*

*And in the morning light, by the paddock fence, side by side and shoulder to shoulder, two tan brown horses stand – the breeze ruffling their black manes, but still, quite still, as if in meditation, waiting...*

Stillness. When thoughts are stilled and emotions are quietened, we can begin to find pure receptivity.

Spirit comes, infusing matter. Matter becomes lucid, reflecting spirit in the ageless language of silence that is transparent, where each thing speaks the essence of itself: *deer, grass, heron, sun, wind...*

The heat in the flask begins to rise again. And it's here that letting each other be as partners takes on a new meaning; *it isn't finally to do with words, but with presence.* We need to go beyond words, to find what has been with us all along and when we're tired, or just tired of speaking, we find this presence – or it finds us again.

## The Question

Finally there comes a moment there is no escaping. It may have been building for some time. The question may even have risen to your mouth many times and been caught behind your lips. Perhaps you sensed the time wasn't quite right – or perhaps you actually couldn't bring yourself to say it. But now it has to be said. The question has to be asked. *'Will you marry me?'*

It doesn't even have to be *answered* now: asking it is what matters. Asking it brings its quality into being. It is the opposite of sitting on the fence and being held in the thrall of uncertainty. We can spend a long time there, like forever, if we choose to. But in the question love states itself powerfully, inviting agreement and affirmation. And that may come inwardly, too, in a voice that is neither yours nor mine, only audible inside where it resonates in the inner air that is like light between us: *'It is'* and now, *'Let it be.'*

## Purification and the Heart Direct

Alchemy pictures this stage of preparation as a rising that is both fire and air. Sol and Luna are both shown 'ascending' with a third feminine figure, who is thought of as a virgin. We can think of this rising as being *towards the heart,* just as there is a descending of spirit to the heart. The heart is our centre, where the worlds meet, but it is blurred through emotion. Any hint or taint of coercion, manipulation or aggression colours and distorts it. For a real meeting in feeling, the channel, like a mirror, has to be clear. This is the purification that essentially takes place throughout the alchemical process, and which I have emphasized in differentiating emotion and feeling.

But it doesn't end here, because what fully comes into being through *rubedo* is the 'heart-mind', which completely changes our relationship to the mind as we've known it. The heart – the intelligent heart – comes first, because the heart is the organ of love, and love comes first. So what we come to here is what I've called the 'Heart Direct':

Heart that is expanding
Heart that is beyond words
Heart that is beingness

and we find the heart going ahead of the mind, bringing us towards rightness in any moment as well as a slow but steady increase of joy. We can say energetically that as the heart takes precedence, our other chakras – our seven major energy centres – change, affecting the entire etheric body that surrounds our physical body. There are levels of the heart, too, which rise into what we think of as 'heaven' (which is also within us).

So for now it's little wonder that when we make love we want it to come from the heart. We want the impulse to begin there, and we find that it does – heart to heart as we stand pressed briefly close. Our bodies follow its red lightning and the light in our eyes echoes it. Sex comes into the heart and that is how it finally becomes love-centred rather than self-centred. Then we discover something precious: *that sex is also virginal*, it is always new, as we maybe sensed it was when it first touched us.

## Being and Becoming

As we accept our own separateness as individuals, so we can not only allow each other freedom and respect in our difference, but we can also *be* with the things we can't solve rather than trying to fix them. We can allow them to be the process they are rather than forcing them into resolution. So we can live them as questions to hold rather than to answer. We each have our own questions that lie at the heart of our life quest. It may even be that our lives are magnetized by these questions in ways we don't yet understand, with circumstances and events being drawn to us because of our specific make up. How much more so, then, do we benefit in relationship by seeing the other – our lover, partner, husband, wife, sibling or friend – *as a being living out a quest* ... and what a relief it is to be seen that way ourselves.

With this way of seeing, our opposition to each other naturally begins to die. We can begin to see the parts we have both played in each other's journey. We can see how we have both been hooks for each other's projections as well as being objects, whether of desire or rejection or both, that mirror our own situation to us. We can see how hard it is for the one who has overtly held more of the shadow, playing the part of separation and distance – even as we have *both* been each other's shadows! We can wonder at how we have both been catalysts for each other. In this deeper acceptance of our lover as he or she is, we are free to take on the qualities he or she has held for us, whether of intimacy or distance – and then to meet in the centre, beyond all this conscious work. This is a mystery which lies at the heart of the wedding.

## The Inner Marriage

But before the wedding we need first to turn back to the inner marriage, for that is part of the preparation, as well as being an ongoing process in itself. For this, we need to accept ourselves in the sense of being 'at one with' ourselves. This can be a palpable experience of presence in ourselves and our bodies. A man who has married, or is marrying, himself is *present* – he is the reverse of the hungry ghost who is drawn and empty, self-exiled in craving and longing.

As another man put it, also in a private letter

I only miss you in a certain way when I'm 'out of myself', and it's as if I just want to keep going further 'out' to you. It's only when I draw back in that I feel it's OK I've heard nothing from you, and my fear that you have disconnected begins to melt away...

The key here (as he suggests) is in *accepting your own energy, as opposed to repeatedly projecting it outside yourself towards the other.* Marion Woodman, from years of thought and psychotherapeutic practice, puts it succinctly:

The withdrawal of the projection that is essential for the achievement of the inner marriage transforms the object of the projection, the Beloved, into a stranger. It is this confrontation with the stranger, with the otherness of the beloved, that creates an 'energy field of love'. When that field of love is established within ... a freedom enters the relationship, which may be quite alarming at first.[4]

What we find here is that we have a permanent contact with our own inner 'other sex' that we have previously projected outwards. We may discover then (as men) that this inner feminine is very different from the sexualized image we have been desiring in outer women—it is an inner soulful (soul-filled) image. The same can be true for women who recognize they have projected their male quality onto men, seeing them also as 'sex objects'. Their true inner masculine quality is also something quite different, and more sensitive as well.

Out of this comes the freedom to love another as a human being, without expectation.

## The Source

Another aspect of the inner marriage that is essential to the *rubedo* is that in becoming one with ourselves *we can be at one with the world.* And can we do this without the true Beloved, however we recognize Him or Her? With the inner marriage we enter the mystery which is *the Beloved in me as me.* And so, as I found myself inwardly stating:

I marry my mind in God
I marry my throat in God
I marry my heart in God
I marry my belly in God
I marry my genitals in God

*In me as me – and in you as you.* For both of us co-exist, then, with this source of greater love. I flow into Him as He flows into me.

*And I felt it then as I sat – a stitching of gold candescence in my belly like a belt of broken light. And its energy was strength and joy.*

With the inner marriage, the famous Stone is also born in us as that quality of permanence as it reddens into its final 'tincture' and form. This is the fruit of our labour, colouring us as it does from the inside with the reddening flush of life.

The door is open to a greater loving, and the *multiplicatio* from the previous main stage of *coagulatio* reoccurs here, uncovering a fantastic source of energy in the heart which is also known as the *élan vital* (vital spirit) or Elixir of Life. This spirit is the heart's fire. It comes from a heart that has the expanse and freedom of air, of spaciousness, of grace and lightness, and a lightness of touch as well. It can laugh – and does – as abundantly as it commits to working for others. *Multiplicatio* is this generosity that links us to the world of service, as we ask, 'How can I help?', and it vitally and wisely locates its source in the Divine, the inexhaustible, the 'gold beyond measure'.

The sheer energy and life of the Divine is as awesome to experience as it is to contemplate, even fleetingly. Where we might have thought of Songs of Praise, the reality is more like a *roaring* that sends a shiver from crown to toe... And we can think of the lives of all those who have astonished us with their energy and dedication, known and unknown as they are, like stars in a hidden sky...

The heat is rising.

## The Wedding

But before marriage can come into being there has to be a wedding – and not the wedding we know, the outer public event we swear by, but a wedding we have forgotten, a wedding *between* us.

What is this wedding? It is a place that we return and return to, and which has its own durability and permanence, however we picture it. It is the presence between us that is more than you or I and perhaps more than we can imagine or anticipate: it is our third body in its glory now, haunting us *with light.*

Heaven and Earth, matter and spirit – because the wedding is in both dimensions we need to see it in both. It is soul *and* spirit, too, and it is a wedding in blood. A wedding in blood means it takes all our desire – we have to really *want* it for it to happen. And it means we are connected to the greater world of the cosmos, both outwardly, living as we do, and inwardly, where the inside of our bodies is connected to the inside of *the* body which is sentient life. That is why the wedding is red – *rubedo* – red for desire and red for life.

Alchemy symbolizes it in the meeting of two roses, in the meeting of the red king and the white queen. We can think of white not only as purity (as in *solutio*) but also transparency. It is a wedding in soul, then, but also in spirit. It is a wedding in spirit because it is ready to be – and not simply by our own will, but by grace. The readiness comes from the inner marriage as its preparation. Alchemy says that it is in marrying ourselves that we become 'royal enough' to be married to another. So the outer wedding can only take place when the inner wedding has already begun. This is what we have forgotten collectively or barely known.

Neither inner nor outer marriage is a single event, of course, but a piece of living art we keep returning to and refining and *being refined in* as the spirit works through us. We could say it is like an instrument – a harp, perhaps – that needs tuning and retuning. 'When was your wedding?' someone asks. '*Actually, we are still getting married*' might be the most appropriate answer. We are *always* getting married !

## Between Us

Here, in the event of the wedding itself, our story takes another turn that is vital to understanding what this particular wedding is about. It is not only about desire and love *but also about death*.

Here we move into *projectio*, as alchemy calls it. It is not the same as 'projection' in the psychological sense that we now understand the word, where I see something in you that I can't acknowledge in myself. It has two meanings here. *Projectio* is literally what happens in the making and multiplying of gold when the red tincture – the powdery distillate of the whole process – is applied. It takes place *before* multiplication, obviously, but here the two stages are reversed. After the birth of the Stone we have multiplication and *then* projection.

At a metaphorical level this means we are passing from the horizontal and spreading out into a vertical, upward movement – like a plane taking off. We are entering the vertical dimension of spirit that also takes us beyond time and beyond the body. It takes us beyond life. As *The Heart Sutra*, attributed to Gautama Buddha, puts it:

Gone, gone, gone beyond, gone completely beyond.
O! what an awakening[4]

It is a process of dying that parallels the death process itself with its gradual withdrawal of energy up the body from the feet before we 'leave' from between the shoulder blades, or at a point above the crown of our heads. And we know it in the flash-glimpse of orgasm, or *petit mort* ('little death'), as we surrender into the great sea in which we move, live and have our being ... because we are dying all the time, and not just physically, *but so we can live in and through spirit*. And our spirit returns to our body and to life, just as we wake up each morning. It is a daily circulation that we live in.

Here it is the death of our egoic separateness, our resistance and our fear. That is what the wedding of alchemy proposes and embodies: *nothing less than the death of everything that separates us from love.* And it does so not once, but again and again.

What are its features? Again, the key word is 'beyond'.

We go beyond separateness, even as we both remain separable.

We go beyond personality, even though we both retain personality.

We go beyond opposition and adversarial thinking to acceptance and then unconditionality, 'a love without conditions', 'a love that *is*'.

*It is the same room, the same day even, but different. You have the same eyes and the bow of your mouth is the same, but our thinking so coincides that we are at moments completely telepathic. We become* **one will.**

This union of wills is the eye of the needle. From here we can go through. Each time we are *swept up as if into spirit* – and emerge as if under a new sky in an unformed land that is ever-fresh and inspirational. And if we make love here? As Chase Twichell invites us:

Bereft of their clothes, two humans
lie entangled in its cloud.

Their bodies saying the after-grace,
still dreaming in the language of the cloud.
Look at them, neither two nor one.

I want them to tell me what they know
before the amnesia takes them.[6]

This is the language of the cloud that is both of unknowing and yet known, known when we are in it. And that is:

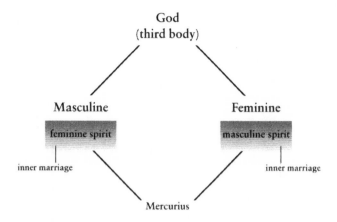

Here the third body we share blends with and reveals itself as the Beloved, as the Divine which holds us. This is the cloud we enter as separable and yet united beings composed of what we bring in our marriage to ourselves, which includes the other we carry within us – you in me and me in you.

As we ascend yet further, and the marrying continues, we become as if archetypal – yet still our human selves. We become yin and yang – yet still ourselves. We become the first woman and first man. We enter a holographic dimension where we become Creation and Creation becomes us, parts which at any point contain the whole, in life, myth and memory, and then finally where we are immersed in the mystery that gives us this union, which reveals itself as *love's relationship with us*. And still we remain mysteriously personal and unique. We are not effaced, only *self*-effaced – just as when we die our essence is alive and blazing, gold, radiant!

This is the radiant body that alchemy names as the state of enlightened awakening. We could call it enlightenment through love – and it is (potentially) there for all of us.

First the marriage
And then the wedding
That is every day
Between love and us.

And this is where above and below meet and marry in us.
Alchemy pictures this wedding as a mutual eclipse of sun and
moon, where even as polarity is retained it is transcended. Man
is said to become woman, and woman man, even as they remain
physically male and female. We come together *as we were created*
– not only as masculine and feminine but in the Divinity which
infuses both of us.

As Philip Wells puts it:

My finger dives into the sun
But does not burn.

It comes out blazing,
Wearing a wedding ring.

I hug you in my golden arms,
Circle you with my love.

The suns spin round us,
Dancing, their purpose done.[7]

## Union

So we come into a unitary state where we find *we are neither
masculine nor feminine but mysteriously the same substance,* beyond
images, even as we remain distinct. We are matter and creation
fused with itself.

As Rumi says:

Don't look for me
I am inside your looking
No room for form
In love this strong[8]

(Fig. 5—H.E's.—near here)

Beyond this? As one Sufi story has it in its refrain, 'Nobody knows, only God knows.' And yet in our own way, and within our own limitations, *we can know too*. We can be part of a new creation where we come together to serve a higher will that is quintessentially creative. We can do this here and now and we can do it, so to speak, beyond the veil, beyond this mortal state. It is a choice we can make and by no means only as a heterosexual couple. Whatever the form of our relationship, we can express the heart of the potential that is sparked in our meeting. And this brings us to the next threshold where the 'I' that we are also needs to embrace and become a 'we'.

## From 'I' to 'We'

The marrying doesn't stop with Sol and Luna, it continues, taking us finally beyond the romantic dream that keeps us isolated in exclusivity or in very limited community. The death of the romantic ideal as we have known it allows something more real and expanded to come into being, and it is this which takes us finally *into the heart of people*, into alchemy's 'heart of the Rose'.

Let me put it personally: it is seeing that the woman I love is in *all* women, while at the same time recognizing *that it is only because she is beloved that I am able to see her in this way*. It is an interesting variation on the phrase 'my wife' (or even more clichaic, 'my woman').

As poet and teacher Alan Rycroft discovered in meeting two

women, without words, eye to eye:

It's like walking on water –
That difficult,
That easy
On paths of liquid gold
Into the alchemy of evening,
The sun of my silence shining
lluminating orbs of your eyes
As my own.
I meet you with no me between...

And in this second woman
Though older than the first
And by the scouring streams of time
Her kindness had been worn down,
I felt it, the very same One
I saw before
Numinous and common as the day
Haunting her eyes also.[9]

His lines reveal the second aspect here: *that we love the one we love in the One.* Again, I cannot do that unless I see you as you are, and I cannot do it unless I acknowledge the Divine. And so again:

First the wedding
And then the marriage
That is every day
Between love and us.

And here, as the heat continues to rise, we realize, as a female guide figure told me in a dream, *'We can love all through our lives and we can love many, many different people. What we have to keep alive is the flame of connection that sees each person we love as Love.'*

It's here that we enter another mystery we can only experience through the heart, which is *that the whole of love is in each person we love*. This is so regardless of whether we have a 'whole' or sexual relationship with them or not. 'How much' we love each person is a distinction and quibble of the mind, not the heart, even as we recognize difference – but difference which is based on individuality and uniqueness, not on competition or reduction. Because there is no reduction here; just as with the coins the queen dispenses in some of the classic illustrations, *there is only increase*. More begets more: the scarcity of love is a mere negative illusion.

So we can take another step into the heart of the Beloved Community, the reality of all of us here 'in love'. We can move into a place beyond possessiveness and fear, even as we may feel these emotions flickering. They are part of what dies here, along with the snake of compulsive sexuality, to allow a greater life (that is love) to come into being.

And actually, it's no big drama or big deal – *it is simply natural to feel this*. Once again:

Apparently it is natural
to feel these things.

We have not understood
how large love is.[10]

It is about loving everyone and being 'in' (as opposed to 'out of') love with them, regardless of convention, comparison or competition. This is the greater loving of the *rubedo* of alchemy.

## Rubedo

**Context:** Synthesis, union, transcendence of opposition

**Key question:** What is your experience of Spirit? What does grace mean to you?

How has love guided you in your life? You can think of this individually and with your partner. Trace a love-line remembering different experiences of love along its thread.

Try the practice of sitting together and attuning to the presence that is more than both of you individually (*see Solutio*). You may also request guidance in this state of attunement or prayer. Be open to how that may manifest – either as something you experience 'inside' (as an insight), or something you experience 'outside' (symbolically or synchronistically).

The exercise that follows is also relevant if you have been widowed.

Consider what you and your partner have represented or symbolized for each other, and what it may mean for you to own that for *yourself*. It may be as simple as doing the accounts or as exalted as playing music.

What does it mean to be married as souls rather than personalities? When did personality become soul for you?

List the qualities of soulful relationship for yourself. What are the key words?

They might include 'self-awareness', 'aliveness', 'realism', 'honesty', 'generosity', 'empathy', 'forgiveness', 'gratitude', 'devotion', 'joy'.

Imagine standing and facing the world together. What (and who) does your relationship serve?

Review your experience of the inner marriage. How close are you to yourself? What takes you away?

Try sitting and consciously bringing attention to the warmth within yourself. feel where that takes you to in your body and being. You may also want to allow and image or picture for this place/area. See if you can see what it is showing you, and what it needs from you.

Make a note of what you find, see if you can return to this place inside during meditation consistently over a period of days, seeing how it builds as you do.

## Chapter Eight

# Above, Below: Below, Above

*rubedo* – synthesis, union
'love's relationship with us'

I am painting in light; the images help people. When they see the paintings, they can look at the beauty around them that they hadn't seen before. What is happening to me is amazing: a complete transformation of mind, will, soul and deep soul. All is part of what we call God: very, very alive and beautiful beyond words. I have joined a group of many thousands. I am no longer battling on alone as I felt on earth; it is simply fantastic to be working in this way.

– Kenneth Butler Evans (d. 1987)

From here, we move in two directions at once that we can think of as above and below.

Above takes another step beyond, expanding into a cosmic dimension that the *rubedo* reaches out into. It touches on what alchemy calls the *conuinctionis solis et lunae* (the actual conjunction of sun and moon), where our lovers are depicted standing above the Earth against a backdrop of stars. In the recent eclipse of the sun by the moon we could all see a greater awareness of connection. We are beginning to see the Earth itself not just as a planet but sidereally, as part of a star system in relationship to other stars, as well as comets and meteorites.

We may think symbolically too about the different line-ups planets make – whether at Harmonic Convergence back in 1987, a major alignment of planets which opened the door to this recent period, or, with the 1999 solar eclipse, the Grand Cross traced in the heavens that also signifies each of us coming more into relationship with a higher will and purpose in our lives. The cross here can be seen as being transformed from the cross of crucifixion into a cross of resurrection and perception through the higher senses. The 1999 eclipse is one example among many that are here and to come, and it exemplifies what alchemy saw and validated as sacred geometry.

We are at the hour of conjunction now...

But just as the 'above' has opened, so 'below' we begin to see more of the reality of who we are and what holds us here. 'Love is the Work,' we can say as love itself expands into all its unnamed shades. And we can say, too, at a deeper level, that love is our existence and our bedrock:

The gold is *under* the black: the foundation is light.[1]

At the same time, because this final stage's emphasis is on the embodiment of spirit, we face the reality of how difficult it can be to love, especially those we don't easily feel warmth or appreciation or recognition towards: our employer perhaps, or our neighbour, or friend who has let us down. It's harder to feel love for those who hold more of the shadow for us and it's hard to stay open when we feel unseen or hurt – and in the shifting, restless movement of life we are all in a minefield of projection where we are making judgements and having fantasies about each other at an instinctual fear-based level. Love by no means always graces our hearts or our perceptions – which is why it is *work*. It is as natural as breathing, but we still have to work to release and restore it. At moments it can seem as if we're getting nowhere. But as something of the Stone forms within us, we find a greater stability. It is an energy that is present, like the light in our eyes. Alchemists say that 'the whole difficulty of the art lies in making the Stone'; we could say that the whole difficulty of love is in sustaining love. *Love is the Stone*, with all the qualities that alchemy recognizes: patience, forbearance, tolerance, receptivity, humility, firmness, toughness sometimes and durability – all the qualities of stone itself.

So it is the work of relationships plurally that we come to here, 'right relationships' as Psychosynthesis calls them, in all their potential complexity. *All relationships reveal themselves as love relationships* if we give them the attention they deserve, as opposed to switching in and out of them and disconnecting as we do. Sometimes of course we do need to withdraw to recover and bring more perspective to a situation. It can be as important *not* to meet. This is where it helps to see love like the stone, 'philosophically', in an impersonal, objective, detached way where the dispassionate heart (so central to successful therapeutic work) is also important. Love is capable of a multitude of forms and shades and each relationship has its own mysterious rhythm and demise.

We can see all that has been said here in terms of friendship as well as romantic love and passion, and we can see how much closer the two things are than they may appear. The main problem in friendship is often to do with the suppression of things that need to be stated and friends can also act like jilted lovers in quite unexpected ways.

So it isn't all lovey-dovey here below – how could it be? The reality of what what we evoke, signify and symbolize for each other dictates otherwise. We may also think of this in terms of karma and past lives (as Rudolf Steiner did). Real as this can be, the process of love has an immediacy that always seeks the present moment – here, now and who we are, rather than rationalizations of any kind:

Quick, now, here now, always –
A condition of complete simplicity
(Costing not less than everything)[2]

as T. S. Eliot put it. This also evokes what alchemists have said about the work 'ending in the simple'. Love in the end is really very simple, and that is its great power to cut across everything, socially and intellectually.

Part of being in the present moment is to do with facing outward as well as inward, which is also part of going beyond romantic self-preoccupation. There's a world out there. This can be a problem for groups who isolate themselves in self-enclosed, cult-orientated ways, whether psychologically or esoterically. But once we face outwards, we go beyond self-love into love from the Self (and for it), the greater good as opposed to the fallacy of 'everyone feels good because *I* feel good'. We transcend mere self-interest and operate in the service of something higher. Stories of this are thankfully everywhere, though as often as not unrecognized and unreported in the gloomy *nigredo* of our news, so we can forget that we live in a world where people do passionate and even crazy things out of devotion to something greater than themselves.

Think of your friends and people you respect for a moment, and consider what they are doing. Imagine them in their work and reflect on what or whom they are serving. Be aware of how you see them and of what images come to mind. I have found this profoundly moving to do. There is an incredible beauty in each of us in our struggle of life and love.

Increasingly as we surrender to life there comes a recognition that every moment is special *and is all we have,* from moment to moment. It is easy to go back to sleep and take each other for granted. But can we remain awake? Our tragedy is that we haven't. Our hope is that we can.

*And as they stand at the height, above where they lay on the grass before, the shielded valley spreading to their left in its grazed quietness and birdsong ... and to the right, and below them*
  *– across the patchwork of fields the world with its ceaseless sound –*

*cars, lit up like headlights in the sun racing in their flat motorway*
*drone over the plain...*

    *And beyond them, in the hazy gold light, upstream from the green*
*and white curve of the river – a single bend of its thick sinuous shape*
*illuminated in pure breathtaking gold*

    *– breath holding, like the sun itself blazing deep into the clear*
*September azure high above, and steady, as they stand knowing what*
*they are gazing at will stay ... for an hour at least without significantly*
*changing*

    *And above the sun a single cirrus cloud hangs sketched in the shape*
*of a swan-white feather*

    *– and below, all the sounds of the world congregate, drawing you*
*down ... near to the lowing cows, crows and a tractor's engine*

    *– as a brown goods train like a giant electric worm slides over the*
*furrowed landscape –*

    *And the sun deepens into deeper gold*
*Until you can see safely into it*
*like a clear burnished mirror*
*as colours start to shimmer round its edges*
*– red*
*green, indigo, blue, mauve –*
*out of the gold that contains all of them*

    *As we slowly turn and begin to walk away*
*Leaving another couple to take the view*
*As we walk in Indian file over the ridge of grass*
*Turning back over our shoulders, and turning again*
*still turning*
*As the sky becomes rose, tinted in soft pink, flushing at its edges like*
*a stain, as if cloaking us in a silent blessing*
    *before the path re-enters the dream of the woods*

    *And it's only finally as we emerge*
*Across the open field with its scattering of heifers*

*That something makes us turn again to see it*

*Round, red, translucent above the horizon*
*In a perfect circle of seamless air and stone*
*– its work of daylight lingering, done –*

## The Sun and its Shadow...

And just as life reveals death (and death, life), so the sun reveals its opposite – what alchemy calls the *umbra solis*, the sun's shadow, 'lunar bride' or 'wife'. One text states simply as well as fascinatingly: 'The sun and its shadow complete the Work.'[3]

It may surprise us, but this is really what we should expect. It is part of thinking paradoxically: if we have one thing, we should expect its opposite or 'other half' in some form sooner or later. We have had a marriage here – an ongoing wedding where opposites have been coming together, opposites of all description, in fact. But rather than seeing the shadow here as oppositional, we are invited to take another step and see it as *complementary*.

The alchemical saying is as clear as it is profound and it has been a personal mantra of mine since I found it. It is saying that without the sun's shadow we *cannot* complete the Work. We can think of this in terms of the gold, too, seeing that gold is made up of light *and* shadow. Why? Because alchemy's aim is wholeness, complete integration, which means inclusion of all our different parts. At the heart of alchemy is transmutation, where things are changed by being included rather than denied. Alchemy believes this to be a fact of energy; we can also think of it morally in terms of redemption.

## The Return of the Repressed

If we leave something or someone out, what happens? They

suffer, they are unhappy, resentful, even vengeful. And what we perceive as their negativity grows. It can happen socially and politically, as we know only too well. And it is the same with parts of ourselves that we banish or repress. They don't go away, they go underground into the basement of our lives. They fester there. And then, as Freud discovered, they turn up again, knocking at our door. Our fear of them, like our neglect, compounds them into monsters. But if we are willing to face them rather than running away or numbing out, as Connie Zweig and Steve Wolf say:

> ...the gold shines through. And we open to the Other – the strange, the weak, the rejected, the unloved – and simply through including it, we transmute it. In so doing, we awaken to the larger life. We sense patterns within patterns. We begin to hear the call of the Self. We no longer simply believe in magic, we rely on it.[4]

This is the essence of the Work.

And at this stage, having been through so much, it can be particularly painful and difficult. What we tend to find here are residual issues – like money, for instance – that can suddenly explode out of the depths, with all the more force according to how deeply they have been held down. Mercurius is down there lighting the blue touch paper, but we don't see him. Our fear is simply that we are going back into *nigredo* – or even, have we ever come out?

Two things are vital here, and both draw on the objectivity the Stone brings as well as the ability to see beyond the concrete mind which tends to literalize everything, and so gets stuck. What this liberates is an appreciation of metaphor. So an issue is never only how it presents itself, it also has an emotional content.

*For him, money, material gold, with its uses and*

*abuses, can represent being sucked in by the world,*
*so he has kept it at arm's length.*

*For her, money represents security and a hard-won*
*freedom, alongside stability and straightforward*
*dealing. So when he is vague about it in any way, it*
*makes her feel unstable and afraid she's being taken*
*for a ride.*

*She reacts, and he feels judged, painted black and*
*seen as 'bad'. He reacts, and they're in: Pluto's cave*
*is open.*

*But as they start to see what money represents,*
*what its emotional content is, they don't have to*
*respond in the same way. They don't have to feel*
*they are attacking each other. And out of their*
*opposition and difference can come learning, strength*
*and respect. `I see you,' they can say. 'I hear you.'*

Furthermore, there is the blackness we all carry in us that can surface at any time. These black holes are charged with pain, they are pockets of negation that can even be psychotic. They don't mean we're insane or destructive (unless we are acting out), but that we are hurting, and hurting very much. And our partner has these black holes too. We need to make allowance for them, to accept and honour them, not to get pulled in by the other, to react, as we perhaps did in the *nigredo*. That doesn't mean we disengage – that tends to create more pain – but what it does mean is that we stay in alignment with our own sense of the Divine, because it is only then there can be healing. Otherwise all we have is repetition and a reactive mess.

While understanding certainly helps here, the only real healing comes from love. We know this in therapy or from hands-on healing; relationships are its real testing ground. No amount of analysis alone changes anything. We need to take care of our thoughts, because the energy of our thoughts has an impact, but it is feeling which moves that energy in a new direction. Change comes through feeling. So the heart reveals itself again as the transformer. *And only love can accept or bless what has never been accepted,* because it has seemed too dirty, too shameful, too beyond the pale. Blessing is a deep accepting, as deep as the soul itself.

The other thing we need for shadow work comes as a consequence. That is humility. For facing our shadow means facing our worst fears and sitting in the place of them.

I discovered this literally sitting one bright summer afternoon in West London, in the gutter. I had been locked out by mistake and had to wait for my partner's return. After half an hour in my car trying to read, sweating profusely, even with the window wound down, I finally gave in and sat outside on the pavement with my feet in the gutter. And for me, the gutter has always meant one thing: being financially destitute.

But as I started to accept where I was, I started to ask myself, 'Well, OK, what's it like here?' Rather than feeling vaguely uneasy as well as irritated, I began to notice my surroundings, small as they were between two parked cars. I looked down at the black tarmac, sticky with heat, at fragments of dead leaves and a squashed McDonald's paper cup. I asked myself, 'What am I looking at?' And I saw what I was looking at was also the Stone, the stone that alchemy says is 'common', in the sense of being anywhere. I was looking at common matter, unpolished and unglamorous. I was looking at the foundation. And slowly, I began to relax. I didn't even care about the peeping, curious neighbour. I smiled towards her instead as if to say, 'I'm fine. I'm in the gutter. It's a nice afternoon, isn't it?'

It's important to see that the shadow can be positive even as its appearance (by definition) seems negative. This is the realm of Mercurius: ambivalent and flexible. Its positive quality emerges through transmutation: that's what transmutation accomplishes. It changes the gutter into the foundation.

The positive shadow also points to what may need to be expressed. Later that evening, I was in the company of Robert Bly. Robert was about to give a talk and was invited to name a quality for the evening alongside the two general virtues that had already been named. What he chose was *fierceness*. It rippled throughout the congregation. We struggled with it in a brief reflective meditation and as we accepted it you could feel the groundswell of the energy in the whole of the church was saying, '*Yes.*'

It's true. We need fierceness. Living in this world, caring about the things we care about:

And still light is bitter and unleavened,
Light is angry, is holy fire,
Full with seeing...

as I once wrote, in a manifesto poem for our time. [5]

The positive shadow can also show up in people who come unexpectedly into our lives. Their message is otherness. Like Mercurius, they are also saying, 'There is also this.' Even their physical appearance may show this. Where what we know is blonde hair and blue eyes, their hair is likely to be dark and their eyes hazel or brown. Dreams can also be messengers of the positive shadow, speaking directly through our unconscious, as can reality in those moments when it becomes dream-like and we find the whole environment becomes resonant, speaking to us like a poem.

## Being in the Flow (That is Mercurius)

Being in the flow is what the positive (or transmuted) shadow brings us. It may even be literally standing in a stream or shallow river feeling the water moving round our ankles and feet. Nature, as Ted Hughes knew, is the book we can read most deeply and it may reveal precisely where we need to reconnect:

> And the incomprehensible cry
> From the boughs, in the wind,
> Sets us listening for below words,
> Meanings that will not part from the rock.[6]

The flow of a relationship may also need to be encouraged. As Thomas Moore says, 'We may honor a marriage's soul by discovering what it wants.'[7] He goes on to list the possibilities, which include distance, closeness, children, 'some brief, some lifelong', some wanting frequent change while others prefer a mould to stay in ... and so it continues. Reading it, we see how important it is to recognize the uniqueness and individuality of our relationship, how we need to let go of assumptions about what it 'should' be. Who knows what we might need? Who is to say?

In future we will see that it is relationships *themselves* that tell us about relationship, rather than authors telling couples. This is very much in keeping with alchemy, which came about as a result of individuals, often solitary workers, comparing notes. There were no colleges or institutions of alchemy. It was not a public profession. It was always experimental and it was marked as much by failure and incomprehension as by success. It had its share of charlatans (or 'puffers') too. It was a soulful business.

Relationships themselves are always experimental and may likewise be marked by failure and incomprehension. Love is an ongoing task, even as our commitment in a relationship or marriage remains. The overwhelmingly simple thing is that while love needs commitment *it only lives and thrives in freedom.* If we are wise then, as well as loving, we will allow the other what he or she needs as far as we can without overriding our own needs. The alternative, through control, creates suppression that splits our partner inside, dividing them against themselves. This will not bring them closer to us *or* themselves, and it plants a bad seed.

Of course it has to be said that, like scorpions, we can also hang on to being in the shadow in a way that denies transmutation. We can all simply revert back to the devil we know rather than address what is at hand. We can be divided against ourselves here between ego and soul. Either way the choice still has to be ours in freedom if love is to be. *Love only lives and thrives in freedom.*

Shadows themselves have shadows too. We live in a world where, increasingly, private lives can be anyone's possession – so what is being put into the shadow here is privacy. The blazing light of the sun has a shadow called over-exposure and what recoils from it is what doesn't want to yield itself to the light. The soul needs pockets of anonymous life where it can breathe – where we can walk out without a name and think and dream the things we dream. As well as over-analysing, we can demand too many accounts from each other.

Another shadow can be refusing our solitude – only to find ourselves stranded in it when friends as well as loved ones let us down. It is only in accepting rather than rejecting our aloneness that we can give anyone the freedom they need – or at least go beyond opposing their right to it. If we didn't there would be no space, and without space, without the spaces *between*, there would be no dance. In freedom, we come and go, moving in and out of each other's lives, at varying closeness and intensity for a myriad of reasons. And even when there's no music, or hint of movement, and the rain is pouring out of a leaden sky, we can see that the dance is always there. We live and love in an incredible elastic web.

Celibacy belongs here, too, as a shadow's shadow. If sex can be the shadow of love, then *celibacy can be the shadow of sex*. It may not be what we want, but precisely what we need. Celibacy can give us exactly the inward connection that we need either to recover or to bring us to a higher turn of the spiral in ourselves. And of course it is a path in its own right, as it has been for centuries of religious people. Nor does alchemy's emphasis on sexuality exclude it. It is there in every *separatio,* assuming a couple stay faithful to each other in the process. We can see it as a pause in sexuality rather than as a denial of it, a means of making a deeper aquaintance with our own sexual and spiritual being as our energy turns inward.

## Leaning on the Beloved

With both solitude and celibacy, when our human beloved is absent, we learn what it means to lean on the Beloved. Many of us come to this later in life and without the work of the inner marriage it can ask too much. We all know of the spouse who dies and the partner who follows, seemingly as soon as possible. This is changing for some of us as we grow more independent, and will continue to do so as we understand that death and separation are there all along, just as Saturn is said to water the flowers in the Rose Garden.

Increasingly as we do lean on the Beloved, a quietness as well as a constancy of life becomes apparent, a realization of how we need to live to sustain our work. It is an understanding of maturity, beyond the fiery flight of the *puer* (or *puella*), but we do not have to be old to be wise. And the more our lives are orientated towards the task we are here for, the more we also have to learn to be with our Maker – whoever that might be.

## The Great Conjunction

It is from this solitude that the greater world opens and we may see the mystery of the above and the below – and the agonizing gap or distance between them, gaping as the sky above a ceaseless motorway hazed in neon. Looking around at our world now (this year, or next, and for as long as we are in this transition out of the Age of Iron), at Eastern Europe, Northern Ireland,

Sierra Leone, Afghanistan, Iraq or wherever the latest conflict is happening, we might wonder *how can the above and below possibly connect?* All they seem to do is pull ever further apart and it all seems so vast. However, this very distance is the space of the choice we all have to make: between the loving world and the loveless world, between trying to be 'in (within) love' and turning away into expediency and barbarity, into the mud out of which we came. We may see then that *it is only the choice of love* that connects above and below as the *rubedo* asks us to, and not only outwardly in our newsridden world but inwardly in all the loveless places we carry inside us.

The world is loveless because we are all here to learn love, and we will go on being in this process until we awaken individually and collectively. Souls pour in and souls drift out, and still it goes on. 'What will survive of us is love,' Philip Larkin said.[8] We know that it's true. The rest is in our choosing and our surrender to what must become eventually a very different way of being.

It may begin right now. If we put love first in our lives, what would they look like? What might it mean for each of us to say that love is our teacher? And that we are all each other's teachers too?

The *rubedo* says it means death – that we invite love's executioner to enter, and that we lose our atheistic and autonomous heads. We might even have to really 'lose it', in all senses. But then, mystery of mysteries: we rise again from each dying, given back our lives ... and *we live it.*

*We enter communion.*

## Communion

Communion is the place the *rubedo* leads us into, extending what we have seen in *coagulatio* and with community. It reflects the ultimate truth of relationship as something that is defined and guided wholly by the spirit. Communion is the alchemical Rose, and in terms of above and below, it brings us further into the relationship between the living and the dead.

Again, the key to the door is love: what else could it be? Here another of love's mysteries is revealed, that when we truly love another person *it is forever.* Whatever we go through, whatever distance and separation may come to pass as part of our journey(s), in the heart love is forever. As one woman, also a psychotherapist, said to me:

> I still love Nick. It doesn't matter that it was 11 years ago or that he's married again or that I seldom see him. When we love, it's forever, you know? But it's only my heart which knows that, certainly not my ego.[9]

Beyond relationship as we know it, then beyond Mars and Venus and all the wise tips in the world, relationship continues like a cloud too vast to pin down. It goes on living and growing even though the form of a relationship or marriage may disintegrate. Perhaps it is really the *outer* form that dies, just as the body dies when we die. We become married *as souls* then, as maybe we have been all along or were meant to be, in our own particular destiny with our own particular trials and challenges. I know that I have found this – but not with *every* woman I have loved. Some have gone, some don't want to come back, some can't come back. So this continuity is not automatic. But it is there in those relationships that reach this stage, whether through passion or age, or both.

We may understand then that we accompany one another all along not just as personalities, but as souls who are growing together. Sometimes that means that one of us is further down the road than the other, in which case that means he or she can help the one behind. We may also discover that much as like-minded souls long to be together they may (and this is a matter of deeply personal awareness) be helping more in the bigger picture by being with partners who are at a different stage.

We can see that love goes beyond sex here, literally in terms of separation, but also as the soul goes beyond the body. We may say that love 'visits' sex for it to be embodied, permeated, penetrated – but then in the end it withdraws and we realize that love *is entirely distinct:* it has nothing to do with sex, or no more to do with it. And this is like death, too.

We can feel this particularly with older people we love as well as experiencing it with partners. Love can be radiantly and very physically present and there is no sexual eros at all, but a *different* eros, that is the heart's, and that is light – 'the light around the body'. Perhaps this is really what sex is, freed as energy.

Again, this is present in the extraordinary charged air that comes into being around someone who is dying or in the event and aftermath of death itself.

When my mother died I was six miles away at the time. We'd driven up that midday in the warm sunlight and she seemed so alive and light, almost carefree. I was the last person she knew who saw her alive.

I was attending a tutorial at my school and halfway through reading aloud my essay on e. e. cummings, I found myself stopping and raising my head as if I was listening for something. Everything was going still. I had to 'step outside for a moment', as I said. As I did I realize in retropect that I was already going into an altered state. The sound of a flute drifted out of the end of the building. I looked up at the sunlight dappling green and yellow-gold through the leaves above me. And then in the distance, as if down a telescope and in slow motion, I saw the diminutive figure of my housemaster approaching. I started walking towards him. And I knew what he was going to have to struggle to say.

That state remained with me for weeks. And later, as I came to sit my exams, which nobody expected me to pass, I knew that help was at hand. I haven't forgotten it.

As I found myself writing years later about a friend, the Atlantean healer Ted Partridge, who had recently died:

You are now
What you always were inside...

Death is an experience that none of us can really know until we're there – that is how it has been designed. But we can feel it, like the sun's rays slowly entering mist, and with particular perception and attentiveness we can observe it too.

Death can bring us to wondering who we are *here* as well as in the life after death, who we have been all along. As poet Frances Horovitz wrote while she was dying of cancer: 'Do you remember my dream where we were all walking in Paradise neither male nor female but all loving one another? I hold on to that.' So do I.

And so, memorably, did Dante, centuries ago in his *Paradiso*, when he saw figure after figure as soft white flames standing in the shape of a white rose, as its petals. This has since been called 'the communion of saints', but Dante saw more – he saw *the communion of souls* that we all belong in, perhaps reunited in the families and soul groups we came from. And this communion, as Dante witnessed it, is by definition with God, the divine energy and substance we are made of that moves the sun and all the other stars. It is a far cry from dressing to kill, or standing in a hall of mirrors. It is as far as we can go.

## Living It

Dante's great poem ends in Paradiso, in the higher spheres. Our task is to see it here, then to celebrate and act on our seeing.

We don't feel connected to everyone in the same way, of course, any more than people feel that way about us. People we

are close to are what I call 'soul specific' to us. That doesn't mean
we can't treat everyone equally. The problem comes when we
start believing that we are the élite and everyone else is asleep.
That is another illusion which has to die here. We might do well
sometimes to think of ourselves simply as the essential beings we
are.

As Ann Evans, widow of the surrealist and visionary painter
Kenneth Butler Evans, says about living this knowing:

My soul
is my freedom

the place of certainty
where I belong
and always was
before I came
into this body

That being
who knows
her transparent part
in the tapestry
of is-ness

There
where silence is filled
with knowledge
and love is normal

There
where enthusiasm
is quiet
and powerful as flame
roaring through forests

burning but not consuming

There
where my body
is a beautiful reflection
of everlasting one-ness.[11]

Alchemy sees us as being part of the Divine while we are here, in this life, with the red warmth of heaven inside us and our blood. It is here that our lives become moved by the whole context of relationship, at every level: with self, with the other, with animal, plant, mineral and rock, with the planet. It is in this process that we recover what alchemy calls the Great (or Cosmic) Stone, which is the planet itself, its process and its purpose – the soul and spirit of Gaia that rises up around us in air, clouds and rain, and plunges under our feet towards its molten centre.

### Service

It is through knowing what we are a part of (incomplete as it is) and what we are here on behalf of – perhaps more usefully – that our lives enter into service. Alchemically, we each possess the tincture, we each hold a piece of the red stone, which informs the quality as well as the commitment of what we do and leaves excellence as is its residue.

As Patch Adams, clown and doctor turned activist, puts it:

...the greatest fun of all is service. Service is the key to wealth. It is the greatest wealth. When you serve you give yourself. And when you give yourself, the pain and the separation are over. Where there was fear, there is now imagination.[12]

In alchemy, the red stone is also associated with 'siddhis' or psychic abilities – clairvoyance, clairaudience, telepathy, distant healing, remote viewing – that we only truly come to at this stage in the context of healing rather than harm, always for others as well as ourselves. These abilities are real and beyond imagination; we may think of them as as an 'ordinary magic' within this expanded and enlivened realm. Glamorizing them is not only false, it misses the point: they are part of our natural sensitivity and are revealed as our sensitivity becomes exposed, purified, strengthened and aligned. This psychic realm is one in which we can all become more connected, just as technology is through the expansion of the World Wide Web.

Red tincture, red stone, red medicine as it is also called – its purpose as well as its essence becomes clear as the old Greek adage above the Oracle of Apollo at Delphi: 'Know thyself.' We could add to this 'Heal thyself', which is what all physicians are also called to do. What marks out this healing and self-healing is *that we know we cannot do it without the Divine*. Any fantasies we have of autonomy are broken glass on the laboratory floor – the vessel we are now in is made of light that we know can no longer simply be our own. It is given to us, and given to be given. It is all given.

## Gold

So who are we here as a couple, as partners, as a marriage? This is where we can stand and face the world together at the same time as facing the Divine, horizontal and vertical intersecting, both worlds in us and with us having become one world. Alchemy calls this summary movement 'the squaring of the circle'. It is where our love achieves stability and durability, and is golden.

Love itself becomes stone: it attains a substance beyond transience and time. We learn this through staying with love over time – older couples, out of the eye of fashion as they are, know something that younger ones cannot, simply because they haven't lived into this substance. Commitment can be an agreement at any stage of a relationship, but it takes time before it is a real bond capable of forgiveness, strengthened by freedom and trust. But we can know it at any stage of life intuitively, as D. H. Lawrence did in his poem 'Fidelity':

> And a man and a woman are like earth, that brings forth flowers in summer, and love, but underneath is rock.
>     Older than flowers, older than ferns, older than *foraminiferae* older than plasm altogether is the soul of man underneath.[13]

His description as it continues is rhetorical, but it still rings true:

> And when, throughout all the wild orgasms of love slowly a gem forms, in the ancient, once-more-molten rocks of two human hearts, two ancient rocks, a man and a woman's, that is the crystal of peace, the slow hard jewel of trust the sapphire of fidelity.

> The gem of mutual peace emerging from the wild chaos of love.

In this we know and support each other as free individuals – as two stones strong enough not to deny each other – free in love as in life, and as indelibly connected beyond our fear of loss and separation in the invisible realm that also holds us when one of us dies.

Fidelity is where freedom and commitment meet, and marry.
    That is our royalty and it doesn't need robes or crowns or finery of any kind to prove it. In our return to Earth we become human, as we are, heart-centred in what we are doing, practising and practising and perfecting.

At the end of the process the flask is unsealed, opening to places, people and things, to meetings and events where we can radiate the light we have and cherish as well as celebrate and encourage it in others. It is a radiance and a sheen, a shining that is the fruit of transmutation and of all our inner workings, alone and together, alone together – and it is where we come home at any moment.

Like now.

### Rubedo

**Try this** exercise with a friend, relative or stranger you are finding difficult to love:

> Bring the person to mind, holding them in your awarenss, and then mentally step back. Observe. Who and what do you see? Notice your awareness of the person in question. Then ask for light to come between you. Don't try and feel anything you can't feel, or attempt premature forgiveness. Just ask for the light. Then see if you can wish or send them blessings.

Reflect on the choice to love in any moment and what

happens as a result.

Finally, a meditative breathing exercise you can do together, 'Breathing into the Beloved':

> Sit and closing your eyes begin to breathe in love, breathing out fatigue, exhaustion, irritation, depression, etc.
> Breathe into the Source of Love and feel what separates you being slowly subsumed into its infinite being and potency.
> Offer up everything that separates you from this Source of Love.
> (10–15 minutes.)

Be aware of your experience, and come back to your body feeling the energy in each cell.

Reflect on a shared spiritual practice together, and what it needs from you.

## Chapter Nine

# In the End,
# the Beginning

*ouroboros*, the great snake
the circle comes round...

When you have come to the end, only then can Beginning
come to you.
– Hélène Cixous

How do things usually end? Relief, breathing out, a change of energy and key. We can imagine a party, seeing people we know dressed up, seeing the familiar become strange again, and perhaps beautiful, in the thick of conversation ... and then we can see them dancing among the flashing coloured lights, some predictably, some self-consciously, some surprisingly, each in his or her own movement.

We can see this whole process as a dance with its own rhythms: the blackening of *nigredo* is staccato, the whitening of *solutio* is flowing, the green-yellow-red of the earthing *coagulatio* is free form – and *rubedo?* Are we dancing in a circle now? It could be measured and graceful as a Sufi dance and it could be a laughing loose circle, too, where we gravitate in and out of the centre, two or three of us at a time, as we go round.

Meanwhile the world waits outside, like parked vehicles in the darkness, and because it is burning and in pain there is a simultaneous ending where everything falls away and we are left with a single overwhelming question: *what stops us loving?*

Fear may be the immediate answer. But, true as that is, why does it sound so unsatisfactory? I have found only one answer to this. What stops us from loving is a question we are not supposed to answer easily. It is a question that is here to trouble and spur us. Because although we live on a single pilgrim star in a vast universe where there are other planets and spheres we barely know of, *we also live in a gap*, a gap that stretches between what we know and what we find. It is not heaven here, or it is only so in so far as we can make it so, in a parallel reality within the suffering body of our existence. We live in a learning curve on a planet of learning we call Earth where spirit needs to meet soul and the heart needs to open.

When it doesn't, we have hell. Our daily challenge is to keep our hearts open in hell, which of course we also fail to do. We fall in the gap. We fail to go beyond our egos, we defend ourselves, we retaliate in all the ways that range from the mechanical to the catastrophic. And yet we long for our experience and our feelings to be different. We dream of love and we yearn for love, determined to be more open and more present next time. So, strangely, the very absence of what we long for is our incentive. It is not only Nature which 'abhors a vacuum' – we do, too. And humanity's vacuum is love's absence, love's ending.

Alchemy pictures the close of the Work in the image of the *ouroboros* – the great snake with its tail in its mouth which is also a foetal image of genesis, of beginning. This brings us round to where we started, but to another beginning which is deeper, clearer, closer, nearer. The difference is in consciousness: now we are changed. As M. E. Warlick puts it, 'The alchemical process is a never ending spiral often returning to a similar point, seen from a higher level.'[1] It is where a new cycle begins.

There is a process which leads us back again. It has to do with where our separation from love started. If you can accept that love is our most natural state, then what we find in all of us is an interruption to that state: a child exiled from heaven and wounded on Earth. Separation we know from birth. This wounding is something else. It is the core wound in each of us which is our deepest pain and hurt, and which is (by definition) least accessible to us and our conscious will. It is the hardest thing to reach because our survival has depended on its being more or less concealed. But circumstances beyond our control, involving others, will reopen it. It wants to reopen because it wants to heal. While it remains closed *we are living in our own gap* – between who we seem to be and who we really are.

In our core narcissistic wounding, the mirrors that faced outwards to our family and our world reflecting our experience turn inwards, withdrawing like the soft flesh of an anemone. We become preoccupied with pain, self-conscious with pain. We try to go as far away as possible from it. Usually, that means we go into the control tower of our minds. And when that wound is reopened, *it seems as if the same thing is happening.* In a flash, the memory becomes the present moment. As quickly, we defend ourselves, we disconnect. We don't want to go near our pain. And so we go on living as before, if we can.

Yet we may not be able to do so. We have a choice between living out of a defence that we know so well it seems natural and taking a supreme risk – to act differently. The risk is that we will re-experience the hurt. But if we let the wound stay open, a skin of light will grow over it. Something will be born, that is the 'child of the Work' that can also reveal the wound as a gift, a growing, an opportunity for the soul that could not have come any other way. You, me, this. Who we really are. And this is where we need our connection to the Source even more, for we cannot do it alone.

And it is here that as we breathe or sit quietly we can find an extraordinary spaciousness in the Beloved – where anger, frutration, pain and hatred can arise and be subsumed in something greater *that is also ourselves* as we breathe and as we offer it all up. This is the adult in meditation or contemplation in the pause that is vital, however we shape ourselves in it, the pause that allows us to be spacious and to go to another level.

This is the emptiness we need to dare to allow so the Divine can enter in – again and again crossing the divide and bridging the gap in every cell of our being.

And the one we are loving? What, in the end, is this love thing we do for each other? It goes way beyond projection and compulsion, and deeper too, into the valley of living soul. The edge where our projections are withdrawn and the beloved becomes a stranger leads then to a further step *where our beloved becomes his or her own essential being.* And there is a mystery here which only duration can know, where it's as if the love we recognize or expect is only a fraction of its actuality, where the older it gets, the more simple and secret it becomes, as we live it, and it lives in us. Our journey with someone we love goes on as life itself does, threshold after threshold, as it may also go beyond its erotic and marital or officially 'committed' form.

Collectively too we may see there is an invitation increasingly in to the Present Moment of Love which means we trust our hearts, and what 'feels right', beyond what our minds may reasonably understand. We are moved—and moved on—by forces deeper than we know, below and above. And we may come to see that beyond even our cherished couple dream, in the end, and in life as it is as opposed to how we imagine it may be, it is (really) *each moment of love that matters* wherever and whoever we are with. How is this moment inviting me to respond ? becomes a moment by moment question, and always in the context of a greater loving that takes us beyond ourselves into what our love is also serving.

At the same time, there is an end to this process and the start of something else: *the relationship that we originally glimpsed.* It is another paradox, which is deeply connected with letting go. Here again it is only when I can really feel that I don't need you that I'm free to love you *and what is between us is itself free to become all it can be.* And that is the thread of gold – electric, gleaming, unbreakable – which holds us.

In *all* our relationships we are constantly letting go into the greater loving, where there is space for them all. This is the clean slate of beginning that we reach beyond our wounding. It is the beginning before the beginning *and* after it. It is the innocence that comes *after* experience. It is a clear mirror of light that we can also see as the third body – feeding back to each of us in its mindful and loving clarity. It is a clean slate, empty with potential, freshness and promise.

In the language of alchemy, it is *prima materia* in its pure state, which is likened to a deep mirror of receptivity underneath our personal or subjective *materia* or stuff, in its turbulence which mists the glass. We are back at the beginning of the process.

We may need to literally 'end' in order to begin. We may need to let go of the relationship we have had. We may need to brave that gap. Within relationship, we may need separation for a while to protect what is newly emerging, fragile and diaphanous like the butterfly freed of its chrysalis shell.

But the future lies just ahead of us, even as it touches the present in its immanence, blue, beckoning, suggestive. And then we may find the butterfly form of our relationship as it is meant to be, freed from the weight of our history as something unique to us that was also there in our beginning. We could even imagine each other as two butterflies in this space, with all of their individuality and lightness of touch, delicate as one quivers at the heart of a flower. It's as if our exploration is ahead of our reality – *where we don't know our relationship yet* in the full freedom of its being or its glory, where its beginning is ahead of its ending, in the ceaseless movement of its, and our, becoming...

# References

## Introduction

*Introductory epigraph:* Fromm, Erich, *The Art of Loving,* Unwin, 1957, reprinted 1975, p.22

1. *See* Ramsay, Jay, *Alchemy: The Art of Transformation*, Thorsons, 1997
2. Jung, C. G., *Psychology and Alchemy*, Routledge, 1944

## Chapter One

*Chapter epigraphs* de Rougemont, Denis, *Passion and Society*, Faber, 1956.

1. Dyson, A. E. *Freedom in Love,* SPCK, London, 1975, p.83
2. Eliot, T. S., 'East Coker' in *Four Quartets,* Faber, 1944
3. From the *Independent on Sunday,* 21 November 1998
4. de Rougemont, Denis, *Passion and Society*, Faber, 1956, p.39
5. ibid., p.45
6. Cartland, Barbara, *A Kiss of Silk,* Sphere, 1959, p.8
7. Bly, Robert, *Loving a Woman in Two Worlds*, Harper & Row, 1985
8. Ramsay, Jay, *Alchemy: The Art of Transformation,* Thorsons, 1997, p.165
9. Hendrix, Harville, *Getting the Love You Want,* Pocket Books, 1993, p.43
10. ibid., p.47
11. Caffell, Colin, *Facing the Fire* workshop programme brochure, London, 1996
12. Kelly, Robert, *Songs* in 'The Blade of Seth and the Peacock's Tail: Towards a poetics of alchemy' in *Boxkite* no.1, Sydney,

1997, p.60

13. Rimbaud, Arthur, *A Season in Hell* (1872) in *Complete Works,* trans. Paul Schmidt, Harper Colophon, 1976, p.208

14. Cohen, Leonard, 'Be for Real', *The Future,* CBS, 1994: see also *Ten New Songs*

## Chapter Two

*Chapter epigraph:* Rumi, Jalaluddin, *Speaking Flame,* trans. Andrew Harvey, Meeramma, 1992

1. Vaughan-Lee, Llewelyn, *The Call and the Echo,* Threshold, 1992, p.73

2. Harding, Esther, *Woman's Mysteries,* 1955, Rider, 1982, p.68

3. ibid., p.75

4. Vaughan-Lee, op. cit., p.93

5. Sohani Hayhurst (Oxford), in a private letter to the author

6. Welwood, John, 'On Love: Conditional and Unconditional' in *Challenge of the Heart,* Shambhala, 1985, p.67

7. *See* Ramsay, Jay, *Alchemy,* Thorsons, 1997, pp.79–80

8. Lawrence, D. H., 'The Stream of Desire' in *Challenge of the Heart,* op. cit., p.53

9. Estes, Clarissa Pinkola, *Women Who Run with the Wolves,* Rider, 1992

10. ibid.

11. Hendrix, Harville, *Getting the Love You Want,* Pocket Books, 1993, p.85

12. ibid, p.89

13. Gurian, Michael, *Love's Journey,* Shambhala, 1995, p.86

14. Alberoni, Francesco, 'Falling in Love' in *Challenge of the Heart,* op. cit., p.38

15. Quoted in Fabricius, Johannes, *Alchemy,* The Aquarian Press, 1989, p.130

16. ibid.

17. Van Morrison' s song title, *Inarticulate Speech of the Heart*, Mercury, 1985

## Chapter Three

*Chapter epigraph:* Eliade, Mircea, quoted in Steve Biddulph, *Manhood*, Hawthorn Press, 1994

1. Fabricius, Johannes, *Alchemy*, The Aquarian Press, 1989, p.143
2. Alberoni, Francesco, 'Falling in Love' in John Welwood, *Challenge of the Heart*, Shambhala, 1985, p.33
3. Rumi, Jalaluddin, in *The Hand of Poetry*, trans. Coleman Barks, Omega, New Lebanon, 1993
4. Welwood, John, 'Disappointment, Devotion and Growing Up' in *Personal Transformation*, June 1997, p.43
5. ibid.
6. Jane Samuels (Painswick, near Stroud, Glos.), in conversation
7. Biddulph, op. cit., p.63
8. ibid., p.70
9. Bly, Robert, 'What Men Really Want', p.11
10. Bly, Robert, *Iron John*, Element Books, 1990, p.102
11. Biddulph, op. cit., p.50
12. Redgrove, Peter, poem title from *The Moon Disposes*, Secker & Warburg, 1987
13. From my *The Christos Notebook* (1988), unpublished

## Chapter Four

*Chapter epigraph:* Moore, Thomas, *Soul Mates*, Element Books, 1994, p.235

1. Hillman, James, 'Betrayal' in *Loose Ends: Primary Papers in Archetypal Psychology*, Spring Publications, 1975, p.66

2. ibid.
3. O'Donohue, John, *Anam Cara*, Bantam Press, p.35
4. Durham, Diana, 'Many Mansions' in *Sea of Glass*, The Diamond Press, 1991, p.127
5. Hope in *Couples*, ed. Sally Cline, Little, Brown & Co., 1998, p.171
6. Kellerman, Stanley, *Somatic Reality*, Paradox Press, 1983

## Chapter Five

*Chapter epigraph:* Pound, Ezra, 'Canto LXXXI' in *Selected Cantos of Ezra Pound*, Faber & Faber, 1967, p.95

1. Moss, Richard, *The Black Butterfly: An Invitation to Radical Aliveness*, Celestial Arts, 1986
2. Carr-Gomm, Philip, 'The Song of your Soul', draft chapter of work in progress (1997)
3. Merton, Thomas, *The Geography of Lograire*, New Directions, 1968, p.40
4. Comino-James, Anna, 'Intimacy' in *Dancing in the Danger Zone: Poems Inspired by Gabrielle Roth's 5 Rhythms*, ed. Nina Robertson, Making Waves, London, 1996, p.50
5. Anonymous; from my therapeutic work
6. Rilke, Rainer Maria, *Letters*
7. Sri Aurobindo, from his epic poem *Savitri*, in Satprem's *The Adventure of Consciousness*, Institute for Evolutionary Research, New York, 1984, p.253
8. Bly, Robert, 'After Listening to the Köln Concert' in *The Rag & Bone Shop of the Heart*, eds. Robert Bly, James Hillman and Michael Meade, HarperCollins, 1992
9. ibid.
10. Durham, Diana, 'Many Mansions' in *Sea of Glass*, The Diamond Press, 1991, p.128

## Chapter Six

*Chapter epigraph:* Hart, David, From a talk given at The Wessex Festival, Blandford Forum, 1997

1. Halsey, Alan, *The Text of Shelley's Death,* Five Seasons Press, Hereford, 1995, p.66
2. Reibstein, Janet, in ' "Knit Your Own Life" – Focus on the Family', *Observer,* 25 October 1998
3. Janice in *Couples,* ed. Sally Cline, Little, Brown, 1998, p.98
4. Hillman, James, 'Betrayal' in *Loose Ends: Primary Papers in Archetypal Psychology,* Spring Publications, 1975, p. 74
5. ibid.
6. Chaucer, Geoffrey, *The Canterbury Tales,* 1387; J. M. Dent edition, 1958
7. *Daily Mail,* 2 August 1997
8. Merton, Thomas, 'The General Dance' in *New Seeds of Contemplation,* Burns & Oates, London, 1961, p.229
9. Michael Wilmott, Nicci Gerrard and the Jordans, *Observer,* op. cit.
10. ibid.
11. Jope, Norman, *Finding Time,* privately printed, 1996
12. Chapter 80, *Tao Te* Ching, trans. Man-Ho Kwok, Martin Palmer and Jay Ramsay, Element Books, 1993; Barnes & Noble, New York, 1995; Vega/Chrysalis reprint, London, 2002
13. Bennett, J. G., quoted in *The Best of Resurgence,* ed. John Button, Green Books, 1991, p.361
14. Thich Nhat Hanh, *Teachings on Love,* Parallax Press, 1997
15. Snyder, Gary, 'For the Children', *Turtle Island,* New Directions, 1969, p.86

## Chapter Seven

*Chapter epigraph*: Part of the Preface to the Catholic Mass

1. Jennie Powell, poet, and see *The Grain in the Wood* (The Lotus Foundation, 2004)
2. Rumi, Jalaluddin, in *The Hand of Poetry*, trans. Coleman Barks, Omega, New Lebanon, 1993, p.76
3. Quoted in Burkhardt, Titus, *Alchemy*, Stuart & Watkins, 1967; Element Books 1986
4. Marion Woodman in *The Maiden King* (with Robert Bly), Element Books, 1999
5. The Heart Sutra in *This Most Amazing Day*, trans. Nigel Watts, Fount, 1998, p.39
6. Twichell, Chase, 'To the Reader: the Language of the Cloud' in *The Snow Watcher*, Bloodaxe, 1999
7. Wells, Philip, 'The Breath Between', Vernon Harcourt Press, 2000, p.93
8. Rumi, op. cit.
9. Rycroft, Alan, in an unpublished poetry ms *At the Steep Face of Your Heart*
10. Durham, Diana, 'Many Mansions' in *Sea of Glass*, The Diamond Press, 1991, p.127

## Chapter Eight

*Chapter epigraph:* Butler Evans, Kenneth, *An Artist's Life After Death*, Ken Evans Prints, 1996, p.65

1. From my *Dream Whispers* (The Lotus Foundation, 2004); verbatim fragments from dreams
2. Eliot, T. S., *Four Quartets*, Faber, 1944
3. Quoted in Fabricius, Johannes, *Alchemy*, The Aquarian Press, 1989, p.198

4.  Zweig, Connie, and Wolf, Steve, *Romancing the Shadow*, Thorsons, 1997, p.50

5.  From 'New Age' in *Transformation—the poetry of spiritual consciousness* , Rivelin Grapheme Press, Hungerford, 1988, p.91

6.  Hughes, Ted, 'A Wind Flashes the Grass', *Wodwo*, Faber, 1967, p.29

7.  Moore, Thomas, *Soul Mates*, Element Books, 1994

8.  Philip Larkin, quoted in conversation with (present poet laureate) Andrew Motion

9.  Anon, private conversation

10. Frances Horovitz in her memorial *New Departures* tribute, edited by ex-husband Michael Horovitz, London, 1983

11. From a sequence about the soul (work in progress)

12. Patch Adams interviewed by Robert Holden in *Caduceus*, issue 46, Winter 1999/2000, p.10

13. From *Complete Poems*, ed. Keith Sagar, Penguin, 1992

## Chapter Nine

*Chapter epigraph:* Cixous, Hélène, *Coming to Writing and Other Essays*, ed. Deborah Jenson, Harvard University Press, 1991, introduction, p.xiii

1.  Quoted in *The Philosopher's Stones: Alchemy as Runic Divination*, Headline/Eddison Saad, 1997

# Select Bibliography

Because there is so much to read in today's world, I have restricted myself to listing a selection of what I think of as essential reading in this area, with books that achieve permanence within change, either as classics or as pioneering works, beside the many quotations and references you may wish to follow up already in the text.

So I would suggest you focus on the following, available either through good bookshops, or from Amazon (especially quick for U.S. titles):

Biddulph, Steve, *Manhood*, Hawthorn Press, Stroud, 1994

Bly, Robert, *Iron John*, Element Books, 1990

Cohen, Andrew, *Freedom Has No History*, Moksha Press, 1997

Cline, Sally (ed.), *Couples: Seen from the Inside*, Little, Brown, 1998

Durham, Diana, *The Return of King Arthur*, Tarcher/Penguin, USA, 2004

Feuerstein, George, *Enlightened Sexuality*, The Crossing Press, USA, 1989

Fromm, Erich, *The Art of Loving*, Unwin, 1957

Hendrix, Harville, *Getting the Love You Want*, Pocket Books/Bantam, USA, 1993

Kingma, Daphne Rose, *The Future of Love*, Doubleday, USA, 1998

Levine, Stephen and Ondrea, *Embracing the Beloved*, Doubleday, USA, 1995

Mello, Anthony de, *The Way of Love*, Image Books, Doubleday, USA, 1995

Moore, Thomas, *Care of the Soul*, Piatkus Books, 1992

Moore, Thomas, *Soul Mates*, Element Books, 1994

Tolle, Eckhart, *The Power Of Now*, Hodder & Stoughton, 2001

Welwood, John (ed.), *Challenge of the Heart*, Shambhala, USA, 1985

Welwood, John, *Journey of the Heart*, Mandala, 1990

Welwood, John, *Love's Awakening*, HarperCollins, 1997

Williamson, Marianne, *A Return to Love*, Aquarian, 1992

Zweig, Connie, and Wolf, Steve, *Romancing the Shadow*, HarperCollins, 1997

# Further Information

'For the Beloved in Air and Stone' was originally commissioned by Martin Palmer at ICOREC/ARC, in Manchester, UK, for the World Forum in Los Angeles in 1996. It was written as 'The Charter Poem' to accompany and suggest a Charter of Human Responsibility then under discussion. Those present when it was read out included Mikhail Gorbachev and Nelson Mandela. The poem was first published in the Spring 2000 issue of *Caduceus*.

A selection of poems that runs parallel in content to this book is *The Heart's Ragged Evangelist*. For enquiries about these poems, please see below. Also for related titles published by The Lotus Foundation *(see website below)*.

For further information about Jay Ramsay's publications, workshops on poetry, personal development and spiritual healing as well as poetry performances, lectures/talks, and one-to-one sessions in accredited psychospiritual therapy or healing, you can contact him at: 5 Oxford Terrace, Uplands, Stroud, Gloucestershire, GL5 1TW, England (01453-759436) or: c/o The Lotus Foundation, 'Lynwood', 16 Lancaster Grove, London NW3 4PB (Genie Poretsky-Lee: 0207-794-8880).

Please check **www.jayramsay.co.uk** and **www.lotusfoundation.org** for current workshops and events in London, and **www.hawkwoodcollege.co.uk** for workshops locally with Jay at Hawkwood, nr. Stroud, Gloucestershire (01453-759034 for brochure).

He can also give talks or interviews on the material in this book by arrangement.

# FOR THE BELOVED, IN AIR AND STONE

ALWAYS AND ONLY THERE IS YOU, LIKE THE SKY OVER OUR HEADS, HIGHER THAN THE FURTHEST STAR, AND CLOSER TO US THAN OUR OWN BREATH IN OUR HEART OF HEARTS;

WE MUST RETURN TO YOU AGAIN.

AND ALWAYS, WE ARE ALONE, EACH ONE OF US, IN THE SECRET WOMB OF OUR LIVES WHERE WE GROW, JOURNEY AND DIE AND ARE CALLED TO STAND  IN OUR OWN LIGHT;

WE MUST STAND AS WE ARE AGAIN.

AND AS LOVE IS THE WAY, MADE THROUGH THIS OPENING OF OUR HEARTS, THE ONE WE LOVE AND CHERISH WITH OUR HANDS IS THE MOST INTIMATE MIRROR OF WHO WE TRULY ARE;

WE MUST RETURN TO LOVE AGAIN.

AND ALWAYS, THOSE AROUND US AND WITHIN US, NEAR AND FAR, ARE THE FAMILY WE ARE CALLED TO BE A PART OF, TO NURTURE, FEED AND SUSTAIN, AND TO LOVE AS WE ARE LOVED;

WE MUST MAKE LOVE ABUNDANT.

AND THROUGH THIS, IN ONE SMALL STEP, WE CAN SEE OUR EARTH AGAIN IN ALL ITS SPREADING CURVES OF

LAND AND SEA, WITH ALL ITS FIELDS AND TREES, PEOPLES AND CREATURES, POISED IN THE OCEAN OF TIME ... AND WE CAN SAY:

*'THIS IS OUR GARDEN, AND IT IS OURS TO SERVE AS WE STAND IN YOU.'*

# B O O K S

O is a symbol of the world, of oneness and unity. In different cultures it also means the "eye," symbolizing knowledge and insight. We aim to publish books that are accessible, constructive and that challenge accepted opinion, both that of academia and the "moral majority."

Our books are available in all good English language bookstores worldwide. If you don't see the book on the shelves ask the bookstore to order it for you, quoting the ISBN number and title. Alternatively you can order online (all major online retail sites carry our titles) or contact the distributor in the relevant country, listed on the copyright page.

See our website **www.o-books.net** for a full list of over 500 titles, growing by 100 a year.

And tune in to myspiritradio.com for our book review radio show, hosted by June-Elleni Laine, where you can listen to the authors discussing their books.

MySpiritRadio